POISONED WATER

POISONED WATER

HOW THE CITIZENS OF FLINT, MICHIGAN, FOUGHT FOR THEIR LIVES AND WARNED THE NATION

CANDY J. COOPER
with MARC ARONSON

BLOOMSBURY
CHILDREN'S BOOKS
NEW YORK   LONDON   OXFORD   NEW DELHI   SYDNEY

BLOOMSBURY CHILDREN'S BOOKS
Bloomsbury Publishing Inc., part of Bloomsbury Publishing Plc
1385 Broadway, New York, NY 10018

BLOOMSBURY, BLOOMSBURY CHILDREN'S BOOKS, and the Diana logo
are trademarks of Bloomsbury Publishing Plc

First published in the United States of America in May 2020
by Bloomsbury Children's Books

Bloomsbury books may be purchased for business or promotional use. For information on bulk purchases please contact Macmillan Corporate and Premium Sales Department at specialmarkets@macmillan.com

Library of Congress Cataloging-in-Publication Data
Names: Cooper, Candy J., author. | Aronson, Marc, author.
Title: Poisoned water / by Candy J. Cooper and Marc Aronson.
Description: New York : Bloomsbury Children's Books, 2020.
Identifiers: LCCN 2019045874 (print) | LCCN 2019045875 (e-book)
ISBN 978-1-5476-0232-2 (hardcover) • ISBN 978-1-5476-0233-9 (e-pub)
Subjects: LCSH: Lead poisoning—Michigan—Flint—Juvenile literature. | Drinking water—
Lead content—Michigan—Flint—Juvenile literature. | Water quality management—Michigan—
Flint—Juvenile literature. | Flint (Mich.)—History—21st century—Juvenile literature.
Classification: LCC RA1231.L4 .C58 2020 (print) | LCC RA1231.L4 (e-book) |
DDC 615.9/25688—dc23
LC record available at https://lccn.loc.gov/2019045874
LC e-book record available at https://lccn.loc.gov/2019045875

Book design by John Candell
Typeset by Westchester Publishing Services
Printed and bound in the U.S.A. by Berryville Graphics Inc., Berryville, Virginia
2 4 6 8 10 9 7 5 3 1

To find out more about our authors and books visit www.bloomsbury.com and sign up for our newsletters.

To the raised voices and young people of Flint
—C. C.

To the people of Flint, and to librarians such as Cindy and
Lynn, who make sure young people have access to the true
stories of our, of their, time.
—M. A.

INCUBATION

It is 2016 and the City of Flint says,
"Don't boil the water"
I return to the city for the first time
since the story surfaced. Riding through the hood,
crossing at the corner of Pierson and Dupont,
stands a string of neon stanchions,
military servicemen, a gaggle of palettes,
a gaggle of bottled waters wishing us well.

My boy posts a picture of his back
bubbling with fissures in an even spread—
having bathed in the city's northeast waters,
the contagion carries itself into the host,
bearing witness to a feast of skin
and other soft metals.

—Jonah Mixon-Webster

Contents

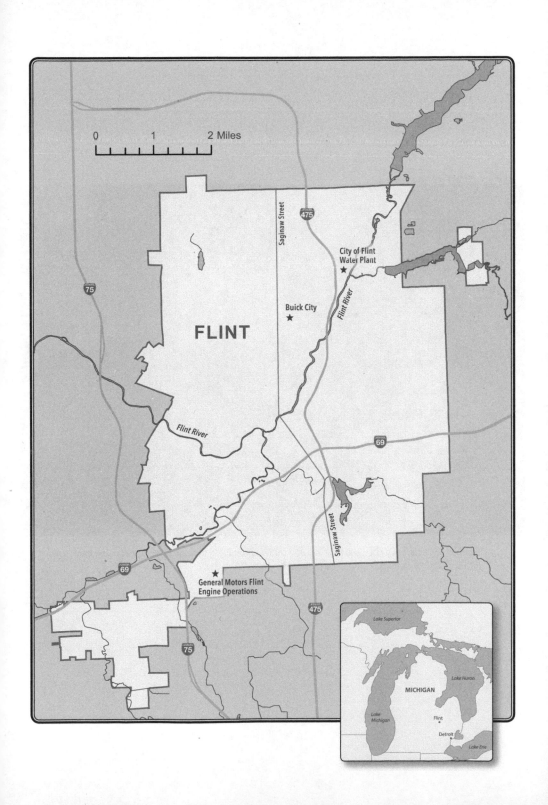

Flint is called Vehicle City because it thrived as a center for building horse-drawn buggies in the late 1800s. Horseless carriages, or cars, soon followed.

Prologue

At Flint Odyssey House on a clear October morning more than four years after the Flint, Michigan, water crisis began, a few members of an organization of community groups have gathered for their monthly meeting. I am there to make a presentation as a visiting researcher.

The group, Community Based Organization Partners, brings together smaller health-related nonprofits in Flint to recognize and advocate for "the community" as an entity to be reckoned with all by itself, like a hospital or a university. The group includes academics, social workers, and clergy, and together they act as unofficial gatekeepers of outside research to be done in Flint, establishing their own community ethics review board. The matriarch of the group, E. Hill DeLoney, has specialized throughout a long activist career in advancing the health and well-being of black youth. DeLoney has spoken publicly a few times about the water crisis, once in 2016 when she sat on a University of Michigan health policy panel. There she described a parallel crisis that ran right alongside the disaster of Flint's poisoned water: an epidemic of mistrust. Flint residents' trust—in elected officials, government workers, scientists, journalists, and researchers of all kinds—sounded as fragile as the shell of an egg. "We need to understand that trust is very hard to get in the first place—very, very hard," DeLoney said on the panel. "But it can dissipate in a matter of seconds."

Flint hadn't started out with very much trust at all. "But when [the water crisis] happened, I cannot tell you how deeply mistrust almost became a cancer in our community. We don't trust anything they tell us, and it's going to be a long time [before we do]."

On this fall morning in late 2018, the esteemed DeLoney has had to leave unexpectedly due to a health emergency in her family. In her absence, two members of the group, Sarah Bailey and Luther Evans, preside. At least four more people have phoned in, including a pastor, a public health researcher, and Don Vereen, the director of community-based public health at the University of Michigan School of Public Health. Their voices rise out of a console telephone on the table.

I am there to describe the book I am hoping to write and to ask for the group's help. I am a native of Michigan and have worked and studied in the state, but I am aware of my Flint outsider status. The room is very quiet.

The woman to my left, Elder Bailey, is a lifelong Flint resident, a church pastor, a community health advocate, and an expert on acute care for stroke victims. I have heard her speak on a panel about the underlying social determinants of the water crisis, where she described the water's effects on her family, her friends, and her own health after she spent eight days in intensive care with a severe cough. Today she wears a jacket, her hair upswept in neat cornrows.

I am aware that race is the "elephant in the room," as DeLoney has often said. She says it is in the water crisis "room" and in the "room" of America. I know that Flint is highly segregated by race and income level. I am white and Bailey, Evans, and DeLoney are black.

But I also know that water harmed everyone in Flint, not just one group or one house or one neighborhood. It harmed people who worked in Flint and lived outside of Flint. And the crisis inspired a comingling of racial, ethnic, religious, and income groups working together. Flint has a very strong community spiritedness that arises especially in moments of struggle, most famously during the brutal Flint Sit-Down Strike of 1936–1937, which led to the consolidation of the United Automobile Workers, the unionization of the US automobile industry, and the conditions that would help build the American middle class during the coming years.

And now I listen as Elder Bailey begins to speak with grave authority, as if uttering difficult truths for an entire community. "You have got to understand that we have gone through *trauma*," asserts Bailey with a furrowed brow. "*Trauma* upon *trauma* upon *trauma*." She is emphatic.

"The water crisis didn't begin in 2014," she continues. "The water crisis began long before that, years before that. It's been a long time."

She was talking about a Michigan law, first passed in 2011,

that had allowed the state to take over Flint after the city slid into massive debt. The governor appointed a single person to run Flint: an emergency manager. The first was Michael Brown. Three more men would serve in sequence after Brown, each imposing a starvation diet of austerity. Flint's elected council and mayor were disenfranchised, denied the right to vote. Citizens could no longer decide what to cut or what to save. The mayor became a figurehead, no longer in charge of anything. All decisions fell to the debt slayer, the emergency manager.

Elder Bailey was referring to recent history, but there is a deep pool of injustice in Flint's overall history as well. Flint was built on car manufacturing—the expansion of General Motors—and it is hard to overstate the winning, all-American spirit of the town at its peak, at least from the outside. Flint had been a model city with excellent schools and a solid middle-class standard of living. Elder Bailey and others in this conversation had lived in Flint then.

"We've seen it in flourishing times," Bailey says. "We were an awesome community. We were above average in a lot of things. We were a model community for many, many years."

Flint was also a leading American example of ignorance, extreme racial segregation, and economic polarization. It's as if every major social conflict in American history crisscrossed in Flint. The city acted as "the canary in our country's conscience," wrote one Flint resident, Ted Nelson, in an essay about his move from Los Angeles to his now-beloved Flint. When GM left, Flint collapsed. That was when, as a Flint pastor later said to me, "The devil broke loose in this city."

Elder Bailey had watched that happen, too.

Economic expansion, racial segregation, industry collapse, state takeover: these had been the prelude to the poisoning of Flint. "This was done to an entire city," she says, "regardless of race, creed, or social background. It was done to the whole city by our state government. And that breeds a lot of contempt."

The previous week, some four hundred journalists had met in Flint for the annual conference of the Society of Environmental Journalists. Some had written stories on the crisis's aftermath. But where had they been *during*, Bailey wanted to know. Absent, mostly, as residents had strained to be heard.

"After they blew it the first time," Bailey says, "by not coming to the city when the city was protesting about this, now everybody wants a piece of Flint."

Hundreds of academic researchers, too, had churned out studies on Flint. They had swooped in and out for their own purposes. What good was any of it for Flint? It felt to Bailey and others in the group as if the city had been besieged, used, and violated.

"We've experienced profiteers coming in and raping the community and not giving anything back," she says. "Nobody really tells that story—about how people enter into communities with their own agenda and never really look at what their agenda could do to a community." One outside researcher—who had won over residents to help expose the water crisis nationally—had gone on to file a $3 million defamation lawsuit against an outspoken Flint mother. The suit had only deepened Flint's sense of betrayal. Months later, in a scathing decision, a judge threw it out, but the sense of betrayal remained.

This sense of trauma and suspicion, while overwhelming on that day, would become a fact of working in Flint, a primary, pervasive truth that I would learn was probably one of the most rational and human responses anyone could have.

Bailey begins to advise me.

"You might need to start your book right here," she says, "right at this point. Because this is the real important topic of the day. What happened here is important for us never to repeat again. This right here is what's going on right now that could be helpful to a lot of people."

Bailey's words hang over me everywhere I go in Flint.

The olive-colored Flint River swirls through downtown.

1

Roots and Margins

Every morning during his last two years of high school, with the slow government destruction of the city's water system as his backdrop, the soft-spoken Keishaun Wade arrived by bus at the front doors of Southwestern Classical Academy in Flint, Michigan, the only high school left in the shrinking city. There, on the dreariest, iciest winter mornings, with windchills plunging below zero and highway traffic droning in the distance, Keishaun and his classmates huddled together while security guards talked among themselves from just inside. The guards decided when to open school doors. They ushered students through metal detectors and examined the contents of every bag and backpack. They held students behind more double doors in an enclosed area indoors. Security chose when to open those doors to let students march off to class. The drill felt to Keishaun more like practice for prison life than a stepping-stone to college.

On his low days, the baby-faced Keishaun, with his mop of naturally corkscrewed hair that fell over his eyes, resented those security officers. He and his classmates grew weary of the morning drill, along with the ice-cold classrooms in wintertime; the holes in the walls and trash in the halls; the renovations that drowned out teaching; the shuttered water fountains and empty water dispensers; the history teacher who turned on the television news, wrote a question on the board, and then played computer solitaire for the rest of class. Statewide, the school had fallen into the category of chronically failing.

Thank goodness for the great teachers, the ones who truly cared. All thanks to Keishaun and his peers, who fought for and won another year of the International Baccalaureate program at Southwestern, the rigorous course of study that readied kids for college. Because overall, Keishaun's high school, compared with the other fifteen schools he had attended across the country, sent a deafening message from the top: good luck with that path to knowledge, those critical-thinking skills, that elusive upward mobility. In the end, Keishaun lost faith that Flint schools cared most about helping kids learn. "It's almost like the school system was putting us down."

≈≈≈

Put down, left out, pushed to the margins. It was an old theme in Keishaun's young life. Both sets of Keishaun's grandparents had left their homes—in Mississippi, Georgia, Arkansas, and Louisiana—as part of the Great Migration to escape the Jim Crow South. They landed in deeply segregated Flint. His paternal grandmother went to Central High School, where two homecoming courts, black and white, featured two sets of kings and queens. His grandmother gave birth to her first child during high school, then had six more. In an environment of scarcity, she found ways to feed her family that landed her in prison. Keishaun's father grew up without knowing where his mother was. He virtually raised himself, with little adult guidance.

Keishaun, too, was born to teen parents. His father never finished high school. Without skills or job prospects in Flint, his father turned to drug dealing and wound up in and out of prison while Keishaun was young. The family became itinerant, roaming four states, moving a dozen times, jumping from school to school, seeking safety and security. Keishaun, the eldest, failed kindergarten when his parents were unable to take him. He learned the role of caretaker for his younger siblings. As a toddler, he peeled oranges and bananas to help feed them. He learned to lead.

When Keishaun's grandmother, a powerful influence, suffered a stroke, he left his family and moved back to Flint to care for her—returning to a city so scarred by abandonment and poverty that he barely recognized the neighborhood. He and his aunt helped nurse his grandmother until her death. It was then, at age fourteen, that Keishaun suffered greatly. His beloved grandmother had modeled an inner strength through her years of racial struggle, just like his late aunt Vera B. Rison, a lionhearted champion of the underclass and a county and state politician. A library in Beecher, just across Flint's northern border, bears her name.

Maybe Keishaun channeled both women. Because on his high days at Southwestern Classical Academy, he witnessed the exact same broken-down school as on his low days. But on those better days he drew strength from what he saw. He vowed to confront the dehumanizing, marginalizing, microaggressive, inequitable, unjust moments at his school. The inspiration drove him to Flint history to better understand the conditions surrounding him. He plunged into piles of books, and one especially, *Demolition Means Progress* by Andrew Highsmith, opened his eyes to a social history of Flint that turned out to parallel his own.

≈≈≈

The Flint River had always loomed large. It squiggled south and west for 142 miles, flowing in roughly the shape of a check mark right through Flint. Forests once surrounded the river, and the Ojibwa Indians lived in the area until the US government acquired all the lands in southeastern Michigan and thereby displaced Native Americans. The white fur trader Jacob Smith founded Flint as a village in 1819, and he and other traders set up posts along the Flint River to use it for transport. The river's first pollutants were introduced with lumber mills built along its banks in the 1830s. Paper mills followed, discharging the waste from papermaking directly into the river. Abundant timber led to the building of horse-drawn wagons, carts, and buggies. Better buggies required iron supplies, and soon Flint filled with blacksmiths and foundries. The city became a capital of carriage-building, then "horseless carriages," or cars.

As gas-powered cars rolled onto American roads in the 1900s, Flint-area investors saw opportunity; they began recruiting car companies to Flint. Soon local industrialists jumped in. James H. Whiting brought the Buick Motor Company to Flint's north side and hired local carriage-maker Billy Durant to run his new company. Durant in turn appealed to Charles Stewart Mott, who had an axle business in Utica, New York. In 1905 he wrote Mott a short letter. "Flint is in the center of the automobile industry, a progressive city, good people, with conditions for manufacturing ideal," Durant wrote.

Mott agreed, and in 1908 Durant founded General Motors. A massive complex of GM factories sprang up on miles-long tracts of land along the Flint River. GM soon grew into one of the world's leading car companies, turning huge profits for its founders and attracting more workers to Flint than any other city in the world. By 1929 the company had produced ten million cars. What was the sleepy city of 13,103 people in 1900 grew to 156,492 by 1930. As journalists then and historians later noted, Flint was growing into an American manufacturing marvel. "Speed, Speed, and Still More Speed!—That Is Flint, morning, noon and night," read a 1937 *New York Times Magazine* story. Flint had transformed from sleepy to modern in an instant. Shiny Flint-made cars sped down streets and whipped around corners; Flint workers dashed to work; speedy assembly lines churned out cars—all while the voice of Flint said "hurry up, hurry up, hurry up," the writer said. Flint was to cars as Pittsburgh was to steel, as Akron was to rubber, he added. Along the way, Flint acquired its name: Vehicle City.

There would be other, less charitable names attached to both GM and Flint throughout the 1900s. These were earned as Flint became among the most extremely racially segregated cities in the country. General Motors's lightning-quick expansion outran the number of affordable houses available to new factory workers pouring into Flint. The first wave of mostly white migrants came from around the Midwest, and in the absence of proper housing, they built their own tents, shacks, and shantytowns around the edges of Flint where land was cheap and taxes were low. Skilled and highly educated auto workers and wealthy executives like Charles Stewart Mott, the largest GM stockholder, erected elegant mansions in verdant neighborhoods closer to downtown. These affluent neighborhoods were homogeneous and highly restricted to whites only.

As more diverse groups of migrants poured into Flint, from the American South as well as Europe, Mexico, and Asia, they faced a rigid residential sorting system that told them where in the city they were permitted to live. Black residents and white ethnic minorities were restricted to two poor, overcrowded, and polluted neighborhoods, with the northern one especially bordered by industry. Soon enough, white residents moved into all-white, working-class neighborhoods elsewhere in Flint, leaving black residents behind.

Throughout most of the twentieth century in Flint, forces both official and informal accentuated racial divides as if coloring with crayon over faint pencil lines. In 1919 General Motors established a new housing division and by 1933 had built three thousand housing units for whites only. Local realtors wrote in sales agreements that white home buyers could only resell to "those belonging to the Caucasian Race." General Motors—or "GM Crow" as it was later called, for its adherence to the segregated Jim Crow laws of the South—offered only the worst and lowest-paying jobs to African American workers, such as janitor or foundry worker. And meanwhile Flint segregated its schools, retail shops, bowling alleys, hotels, taverns, and cemeteries. By the end of the 1930s, Flint was the third most racially segregated city in the country and the most racially segregated city in the North.

Then the federal government literally colored the areas within the racial lines of Flint and elsewhere through a process known as redlining, named for a mapping system that graded neighborhoods on a scale from "A" to "D." The "Ds" were the least desirable neighborhoods and were colored red. If you lived in one of those, you were not eligible for a home loan insured by the federal government. All black neighborhoods in Flint were redlined as unsafe for home loans.

Still, African Americans in the South seeking decent-paying jobs in the North came to Flint in record numbers, increasing Flint's black population from about 6,500 in 1940 to 34,500 by 1960, a quadrupling. The color lines—the physical racial boundaries—remained as fixed as prison walls. Black newcomers were restricted to the two neighborhoods known as St. John Street and Floral Park, where there would be no government-secured loans to improve or expand housing. City inspections in the 1950s found substandard housing, extreme overcrowding, and landlords who took advantage by inflating rents.

The environmental consequences could only be guessed at, though the St. John Street neighborhood in particular was an island bordered by industry. A 1966 report by the state's Civil Rights Commission featured a black businesswoman and longtime resident of Northeast Flint complaining of smog. She said the toxic emissions from a nearby foundry were causing damage to property. A public health official had told her the area had the city's highest incidence of cancer. She said she and her husband had suffered from throat cancer. She had undergone surgery, but his had already killed him.

By the 1960s, civil rights leaders in Flint began fighting for integration. One of the first black mayors in the US, Floyd J. McCree, was elected in 1966 in Flint, which became the first city in the nation to pass by popular vote an open housing referendum two years later. Now African American residents were free to live anywhere. But as they moved into white neighborhoods, whites in turn sold their homes and fled, often to white suburbs in what was known as "white flight." Or, as activists often noted, integration was "the period between the moving in of the first Negro in a neighborhood and the exit of the last white." Integration in Flint had achieved only a re-sorting, or resegregation. The invisible wall had moved—erected now between an increasingly black-majority city surrounded by white-majority suburbs.

≈≈≈

Already, during the 1940s and 1950s, General Motors had begun building new factories outside of city limits. Flint kept supplying GM's water and infrastructure needs because it needed GM and its tax revenues. Without GM, one city official said, Flint wouldn't exist. Flint tried to widen its boundaries to keep up with GM's sprawl. But the mostly white suburbs, with their own new infrastructure, were growing territorial. They wanted GM's tax revenues, too. Flint found itself landlocked by white suburbs more interested in their own improvement and survival than in the old city, now majority black, they had left behind.

Difficult economic times in the US during the 1970s hit Flint especially hard. An energy crisis and economic recession prompted GM to cut its workforce by nearly half across the US. In the Flint area, layoffs and plant closures also meant half of GM employees lost their jobs. This decade was a particularly bad spike during thirty years of decline.

Between 1955 and 1987, the carmaker eliminated thirty-four thousand jobs in the region. As GM contracted, the Vehicle City began a parallel decline toward disaster. GM jobs in Flint dropped from 80,000 at their peak to fewer than 5,000 today, and for every GM job there were likely ten more that disappeared with it if you included all of the related jobs that supplied the parts for car making.

Losing jobs also meant losing people. Between 1960 and 2015, Flint's population dropped by half, from nearly 200,000 to fewer than 100,000. Increasingly, those who could afford to go left and Flint's tax base withered. By the early 2000s Flint was broke, unable to fix up its schools, roads, sidewalks, or sprawling, dilapidated water distribution system, built for a much larger city. And, instead of helping, the State of Michigan cut off tens of millions of dollars in revenue-sharing that had once gone to central cities like Flint.

Then, in 2011, the state sent in Flint's first emergency manager, the person whose job it was to cut costs without weighing the possible hardships to Flint residents. Like the real estate practices of the 1920s, the government redlining of the 1940s, and the white flight of the 1970s, the new emergency manager law had an unequal effect on African Americans. Black residents in Michigan had a 50 percent chance of living in a city controlled by an emergency manager; white residents had only a 10 percent chance.

Under the state's cost-cutter, a slow and steady marginalization of a community had been made complete.

≋

Keishaun Wade was overwhelmed. The intricate details of his early life—the states, the schools, the homelessness—rested on a history that shaped Flint today, down to his very own high school, his own family, himself. His history was a version of many such histories in Flint. Lack of opportunity led to disempowerment, which often led

to a life on the margins. "When you have a community where oppor-
tunities are stripped away, it's easy for those communities to become
marginalized," he said. "That is how the water crisis happened."

History, and especially the racist policies that governed black life
in Flint, had helped to explain the roots of the Flint water crisis, at
least to Keishaun Wade. A state panel on civil rights later agreed.
The push of a button triggered the start.

A workman stands atop a portion of the Karegnondi Water Authority pipeline, built to bring Great Lakes water directly to Flint, bypassing Detroit. While the pipeline was being built, authorities decided to use and treat water from the Flint River for drinking.

2

Pure, Natural, Mineral

In early March of 2014, the amiable and pale-faced mayor of Flint, Michigan, Dayne Walling, strode to a lectern at city hall to deliver his annual State of the City Address. A standing ovation rose and tapered to quiet as he began. "Well thank you all," he said with a wave and smile as the chamber settled into hard seats. "Good afternoon and welcome." Local TV cameras clicked on to record.

A high school color guard and a pastor's convocation lent ceremony to the moment, and the prayer especially suggested the need for miracles to fix Flint's epic burdens. The city had garnered so many "worst of" rankings that local writers had compiled an anthology of essays with the title *happy anyway*. Their beloved town was one of the most destitute, sickly, violent, poorly run, abandoned, and "miserable" cities in the country, the rankings said. A headline writer had harshly branded Flint "Murdertown, U.S.A." And in some corners of town, Flint looked like a ghost town, with whole city blocks resembling ruins and six thousand abandoned properties needing demolition. Flint's ancient infrastructure also verged on collapse. In all, fixing Flint meant pushing a rock up a mountain or, in the birthplace of General Motors, towing a rusted and broken-down old Buick up a hill.

Walling appeared mayoral in his blue blazer, tight haircut, and American flag pin on his lapel. The council looked like elected officials who listened to voters and advised the mayor. But not one of them held any sway. The actual lone authority—Flint's viceroy, or emergency manager—was Darnell Earley, a sober-looking man and the only African American to serve among four successive emergency managers. He sat quietly in the front row, arms and legs crossed, a pocket square in his breast pocket. His mustache and goatee were graying unevenly, forming a white circle around his mouth. Appointed by the governor, he had one mission only: to cut Flint's costs and add to its revenues until the two columns came out even. There was no column to measure the pain or suffering people might endure along the way. The law addressed a math problem. Earley's job was to solve it by balancing the budget. That was all.

The mayor spoke with enthusiasm about Flint's greatest resource: its 99,000 resilient people. Yes, the loss of industry and its tax base, along with the radical slashing of city services, had nearly crippled Flint. But he called upon Flint's citizen volunteers, his "fellow Flintstones," to fill the void. Together they would reduce violent crime, eradicate blight, mow lawns, pick up trash, paint over graffiti, and board up abandoned houses. It would be, to quote the theme of his speech, a "year of service and action."

The mayor's written talk was about thirty-six pages long, beginning with seven double-starred highlights and a detailed two-page

outline. But the topic that would catapult the city toward disaster—
the decision that would intimately touch every fellow Flint resident
every single day of the year—did not appear until page twenty-nine.
It concerned the Flint River, a natural resource right in Flint's
midst. Once a soup of industrial pollution and human dumping,
the river had undergone dramatic renewal in recent years, attracting
blue herons and bald eagles once again, and drawing local birders,
kayakers, and swimmers to its waters.

Now the Flint River figured into a plan to save money.

For the past fifty years Flint's drinking water had been drawn
from Lake Huron, one of the Great Lakes that every Michigan student remembered by the acronym HOMES: lakes Huron, Ontario,
Michigan, Erie, and Superior. The string of connected lakes formed
one of the largest bodies of fresh water in the world. The lake water
was pumped and treated nearly at the source by the City of Detroit
before it hurtled by pipeline to Flint.

Going forward, though, a new roughly seventy-mile pipeline was
to be built to draw raw water from Lake Huron, the one hugging the
eastern shore of mitten-shaped Michigan. The water would be delivered directly to Flint, bypassing Detroit, which had been charging
Flint residents more and more for their tap water. With the new
pipeline, Flint would set its own rates. Residents would save money,
at least in the long run, enthusiasts said. That part of the plan—
creation of the Karegnondi Water Authority, the name of which was
derived from a Native American word first used by the Wyandot
people to name Lake Huron—had been formulated years earlier.

But first, while the new pipeline was being built, starting the
next month, Flint would dip its drinking straw into the Flint River.
Flint would drink river water processed by its own water treatment

plant until the new pipeline was complete, a project estimated to take anywhere from two to three years.

Honestly, there would be a taste difference, the mayor said, with river water containing more minerals. But river water would be "properly treated" and "lightly fluorinated," he added, holding thumb and forefinger in the air like a wine taster.

"So later this spring," Walling said in a light tone and with an ironic smile, "we will all be drinking Pure Flint, Michigan, Natural Mineral Water." The audience chuckled. It sounded preposterous. The river had a notorious history of heavy pollution. It seemed to

On April 25, 2014, officials gathered at the Flint Water Treatment plant to switch from Great Lakes water, treated by Detroit, to Flint River water. "Here's to Flint," the mayor said. Howard Croft, Flint's head of public works, raises a glass in the foreground.

defy logic or common sense. And yet in the mayor's telling the idea sparkled like champagne.

The following month, on April 25, 2014, in an official ceremony at the Flint Water Treatment Plant, a small crowd, nearly all of them men, issued a countdown. Then Mayor Walling pressed a black button on a cinderblock wall, switching off the flow from Lake Huron and unleashing that of the Flint River. The assembled officials held up their plastic glasses for an infamous toast: "Here's to Flint," Walling said, and the crowd echoed, "Here's to Flint" and "Hear, hear."

And suddenly, river water streamed into the city's musty old water treatment plant, which had been cleared by the state to treat raw river water for drinking. Then the treated water moved along. It gurgled into Flint's underground waterworks, pulsed through hundred-year-old water mains, and then dispersed through residents' indoor plumbing. It circulated through water heaters and washing machines, spurted out of faucets and shower heads, sloshed into toilets, bathtubs, and sinks. It cascaded into kitchen pots of pasta and potatoes. It topped off formula in baby bottles and poured into pitchers to make Kool-Aid as the days grew warmer. It splashed into the water bowls of cats and dogs. River water filled fish tanks, fed houseplants, and flooded backyard kiddie pools.

Within days, with no ceremony at all, the citizens of Flint registered alarm: this water was unfit for any living thing. Less than two weeks after the switch, resident Lathan Jefferson, a man in his sixties who drove an ice-cream truck, watched his water turn a rust-colored brown. Soon he had a skin rash and went to his doctor. The doctor said he suspected the water to be the cause. Jefferson sat down with his cell phone and landline, determined to manage callbacks and being placed on hold until he made progress. He called the US Environmental Protection Agency in Washington, DC. Washington sent him to an office in Atlanta, which sent him to Chicago. He called the EPA Region 5 office in Chicago, which oversees the water in the Great Lakes.

"Mr. Jefferson said he and many people have rashes from the new water," reported an EPA supervisor, Jennifer Crooks, in a May 15 email to her superiors. "He said his doctor says the rash is from the new drinking water."

A few days later in late May, the *Flint Journal* reported that several water complaints had been lodged with the state. One resident told a reporter the water was "murky or foamy," while another said it smelled strongly of chlorine. On June 2 a local NBC reporter, seeking to interview Flint residents, set out for a Family Dollar store in Flint to check on sales of bottled water. Just inside the front door, the camera lingered on a long beverage dolly stacked with cases of bottled water. Within five minutes sixteen cases disappeared, or 384 bottles of water sold to residents afraid to drink from their taps.

"It smells and tastes bad," resident Senegal Williams told the reporter. "It's not proper for people to be drinking, man. If I can *smell* it?" The harm was evident, unquestionable. "This is not a big debate," he said. "This is nothing that nobody can't figure out."

The reporter took the critical accounts he'd gathered to Flint officials, then paraphrased for his viewers the city officials' general response: "The water is perfectly safe for everybody to drink."

A few days later, on June 8, during the public comment part of a regular city council meeting, Flint citizens began to speak more forcefully about water. They represented the full spectrum of Flint's diversity. Some were meek and slow, inching toward the microphone, apologizing for their lack of expertise. Others spoke with authority or anger. And frequently members of Flint's black clergy appeared with fiery reports from their congregants. In response, Eric Mays, a contrarian councilman with a deep baritone voice, would often affirm their words.

At the June meeting Reverend Barbara Bettis approached the lectern and adjusted the mic to her small stature. Bettis, in her seventies, was dressed in white garments: a white dress, white coat, and white head scarf, all set off by wraparound dark mirrored sunglasses. She had never spoken to the council before, and she began with a personal story. She had been late paying her water bill so her water had been shut off. She went to city hall and paid $450 to have it restored.

"I thought I was paying my *bill*," Bettis said, with a distinctive reverend-like cadence and vocal rasp, "but I found out I was paying my *deposit*. So I was still in the *hole* with the water bill for the next *month*. Yet!"

"Right," murmured the stentorian voice of Councilman Mays.

Bettis paused. "I don't know how a senior citizen, with less than $758 a month coming in, with a gas bill in the wintertime of four and five hundred dollars a month, and then a water bill of five or six hundred dollars . . ." The chamber seemed to calculate the math along with her.

"This is really . . ." she trailed off. "I don't know what you'd call it."

Some 41 percent of Flint residents fell below the poverty level set by the US government. Yet Flint's water and sewer rates had shot up astronomically. Flint residents now paid the highest water rates in their county. A national study, by the public interest group Food and Water Watch, found Flint's water rates to be the highest in the US. Many in Flint simply could not pay.

They would need to find a way, because the city, under the control of Emergency Manager Earley, was also cracking down: shutting off water for nonpayment of bills, charging ever-higher reconnection fees, and placing water liens on homeowners who couldn't pay—their unpaid bills were simply added to their property taxes for later collection. If they couldn't pay their taxes, they could lose their homes.

The city hired a former police official as a water enforcement officer to catch and prosecute people who might tamper with their water meter or otherwise try to access Flint water for free. Non-payment of water bills could rise to the level of a criminal offense. The city considered the problem "massive," and in September of 2014 they arrested and jailed seven water violators, held a press conference with the county sheriff and prosecutor, and furnished the offenders' names to the public.

"I can't even find the *words* to say what you'd call it," Bettis said.

"Right," Mays said.

"Besides *oppressing the poor!*" Bettis called out, elongating the last words for emphasis. *"Oppressing the poor people!"*

"Right," Mays said.

"You *know* we cannot pay these bills!" Bettis said. It would be years before the State of Michigan would offer residents some form of restitution.

As her voice rose Bettis caught herself. "I'm going to tone it down a bit."

"Go ahead," Mays said, and others in the crowd urged her on.

"This water is not good to drink!" she declared. "I pray and ask the Lord to *heal* this water because this is not good water! I say it is *not good water*! We shouldn't even be *drinking* it. It *stinks* and it's *nasty*!"

An energized crowd cheered and applauded.

"Thank you," said Scott Kincaid. The city council president, who was white, spoke softly. He was frustrated. He had argued strenuously against using the river. He had skipped the ceremony at the water plant in protest. He loathed the emergency manager law. But under that law he was powerless. "Next speaker?"

Many residents spoke publicly and often about the foul qualities of Flint River water. Resident Derico Cooper displays a bottle of his brown tap water at an event, Healing Stories on Racial Equity, held in early 2015.

3

"The Water Is Biting Them"

In late summer of 2014, Nayyirah Shariff discovered by accident, while reading the local newspaper online, that the city had announced a boil water advisory. She had stumbled across a story and a grainy map. She zoomed in and studied the low-resolution graphic, the shading, the street names. Did she live in the shaded area? She did! Why hadn't anyone told her? This was day three of the advisory after a swath of Flint's west side tested positive for total coliform bacteria. How much care or concern had gone into notifying the public when Shariff, a sophisticated political activist who kept up with the local news, didn't know? Her neighbor had four small children. Did they know? Shariff alerted them. Boil to drink, to bathe, and to brush your teeth, she warned. Boil for any use besides flushing the toilet.

Since the switch, the properties of Shariff's water had shifted like stormy weather. It smelled like sewage or rotten eggs and looked pale brown like chicken broth or whiskey. Along with everyone else, she paid a premium price—for what should have been premium water. Instead, the advisory told her, the liquid that spilled from her tap might contain human or animal feces.

It was a shock to Shariff, a thirtysomething woman who wore colorful head scarves and bold jewelry as she battled injustices throughout Michigan, heckling the governor on the street one day,

Nayyirah Shariff fought a Michigan law that allowed a single financial overseer, appointed by the governor, to take over Flint. "There've been wars won and lost over democracy," she said. "With the stroke of a pen . . . we lost it here in Michigan."

sitting on a university panel the next. She had an encyclopedic understanding of the emergency manager law and believed it had led directly to Flint's sky-high water rates. The law had had a racially and economically unequal effect in the state, she knew, and she said so often: "If you are a poor community you can lose your democracy, not because of a war—like there've been wars won and lost over democracy—but with the stroke of a pen. And we lost it here in Michigan."

Now rotten water had crept into her own home. She filled the colossal twenty-four-quart pots she happened to keep for food canning and set them on the stove. It took an hour or so for the pots to boil, and Shariff felt like a homesteader. She had never liked roughing it. Her mother had grown up without running water. Shariff called her. "How did you deal with that?" Shariff asked her. "I'm having a breakdown."

Throughout the summer and fall of 2014, many Flint residents detected that their water, already as expensive as crude oil, might also be foul and toxic. Reverend Bettis had been among the first to publicly call the water "nasty" in early June. Three boil water advisories, in August and September, gave credence to a rising wave of public dissatisfaction. As the year progressed, grievances about water prices and shutoffs multiplied into empirical findings about water quality. And the sensory evidence about the water— what residents heard, saw, smelled, touched, and tasted—spilled into the open at council meetings, in local newspaper and television accounts, in letters to the editor, and on Facebook feeds all over Flint.

A shared vocabulary of bad water emerged. The mayor's Pure Flint, Michigan, Natural Mineral Water smelled like excrement. It felt like burning on the skin. It looked cloudy, contained a black residue, and left a filminess on the tongue. One resident drank it and vomited. Another took a sip and gagged. A third was so repulsed by the smell she couldn't bring a glass of water to her lips. It was fishy, putrid, and discolored, yellow like urine, brown like tea, smelly like a sewer. It was gold, dirty, dingy, and stinky. Use a facecloth at night and find the dried cloth rigid and brown in the morning. "Sort of like funk meets chlorine," said one Michigan State University professor of public health, a Flint resident. "Like imagine you just left a sporting event and instead of taking a shower you put on cologne? It was sort of like chlorination over the top of funk."

The response to these vivid citizen descriptions often came in the official language of measurements, standards, and regulations. Citizen worries, officials suggested, were unfounded. "It's a quality, safe product," Mayor Walling told the *Flint Journal* in a June 12 story that reported on the public outcry at the council meeting. "I think people are wasting their precious money buying bottled water."

≈≈≈

Often it was women who first noticed and spoke up. Women and mothers spent more time in kitchens filling pots for boiling or drawing baths for their young. Mothers examined skin rashes and often noticed first when behavior changed. Over time, parents' personal anxieties pushed them toward politics while activists discovered that their abstract warnings now visited them personally in their homes. Over the course of months and years, residents transformed themselves. Flint moms took up science, a poet became a lobbyist, parents shut down a freeway. Many called themselves water warriors and met for the first time at city hall.

"Good evening," said Shalana Jackson, a twenty-seven-year-old mother of five who addressed the council during public comment at a meeting months into the switch. She was not among the first residents to complain to the council, but her testimony offered the most vivid details. She wore her brown hair pulled straight back and clasped her hands in front of her.

"My water comes out of my faucet smelling [like feces]," Jackson said. She was pulling out "gobs" of her own hair every day and her hairline was receding. She showered infrequently because the water burned and caused a rash. She lifted a pant leg to display the persisting red marks. People in council chambers leaned forward to take a look.

"When I'm in the shower I feel like acid is being poured on my skin," she said. "My two-year-old son cries and screams bloody murder every time he's in the bathtub. We all get out looking like lobsters. Like we just got put in boiling water. And we haven't. My daughters tell me the water is biting them. Four and six. The water is biting them."

Fathers, too, described third-world-ish moments. The July 28 city council meeting brought an anguished man in a crisp suit and tie, Johnny Muhammad, to council chambers. He pulled a cell phone from his breast pocket and opened it to a video he had recorded earlier in the month. He let council members pass the video around for viewing while he spoke. A water main had ruptured just before the July 4 weekend and he was unable to reach officials to fix it, he said. "As [the water] ran for a week I was out of water," he told the council. "I had to go down and dip water out of there to flush my toilet, to get water to bathe myself and my three young children, to wash dishes." The force of the gushing water had apparently collapsed the paved surface of the street. And the water he carried home for use in the toilet left a stain.

There would be 450 such water main breaks in 2014 alone due to acidic river water wearing down pipes, the County Health Department later explained. The broken mains increased the chances of water contamination, spilled vast torrents of Flint water, and disrupted service to customers like Muhammad.

Over time, July 4 of 2014 became a river water reference point. That was the day Bishop Bernadel Jefferson enjoyed the holiday at her daughter's home with her extended family. Seven or eight children and grandchildren filled a wading pool from the garden hose and jumped in. They sprayed each other with the hose and splashed around for hours. Only at nightfall did they make a discovery. "I got bumps on me," called out Marquez, Jefferson's son, a preteen then. "It's super itchy."

Each child had broken out in a stinging rash, all on different parts of the body. They thought it was a disease. Jefferson suspected the water. She had been hearing complaints at her church.

A regal-looking woman with gold-tipped hair, Jefferson, like Shariff, had seen the crisis coming. Retired from General Motors, she was short in stature but long on fight and tenacity, she liked to say. She was grateful for her gift of outspokenness—her "big mouth," as she put it. She had opposed the state's emergency manager law from its earliest days. She, Shariff, and others had in 2012 gathered enough signatures statewide to put a referendum on the November state ballot that would overturn the emergency manager law. Voters overwhelmingly agreed and struck it down. But a few weeks later the lame duck legislature passed a new version of the same bill and the governor signed it.

Jefferson also held sway as pastor of the Faith Deliverance Center in downtown Flint and was a leader in a socially conscious group of clergy, the Concerned Pastors for Social Action. She made protest

Bishop Bernadel Jefferson, an early critic of the emergency manager law, helped to establish the first water drop-off and pickup site in Flint. Here she speaks out at an event, Healing Stories on Racial Equity, in early 2015.

a part of the family culture, taking children and grandchildren with her to events around the state and country.

She had watched the emergency manager law take the stuffing out of Flint. City assets were sold off, labor contracts undone, pensions reduced, departments cut, and some seventy police and fire personnel let go. All while the city, under the lone emergency manager, who answered to the governor, charged more for nearly every city service. It was as if the state thought it could find the money to fix Flint in the pockets of its destitute residents. It made no sense.

They couldn't pay more. And now the water was giving Jefferson's children and grandchildren rashes. For Jefferson, too, the political had turned personal.

At the August 25, 2014, meeting of the Flint City Council, an activist friend of Jefferson and Shariff named Claire McClinton, a retired General Motors worker and union advocate, had an announcement to make. McClinton had been an unofficial mentor to protesters, passing along wisdom about organizing and peaceful action, which had earned her a nickname she disliked: "Mama Claire." On this night a pale pink bandana covered her hair, and the slender fingers of one hand rested on the neck of the microphone as she ticked off a no-nonsense list of grievances. "More and more residents are living without water in this city," McClinton said.

A neglected mobile home park on Flint's east side had had its water turned off after the absentee owner failed to pay the bill. Renters, through no fault of their own, were left without running water, so they pumped water from a well at a nearby cemetery. The Mission of Hope drop-in homeless shelter on Flint's north side, the only daytime shelter for the homeless in the county, had also had its water shut off.

In response, McClinton, Shariff, Jefferson, and others had begun delivering bottled water to homes where taps had been shut off. Now the group was setting up the city's first emergency water relief site. Residents would be able to drop off or pick up bottled water according to their ability to give or need to take.

McClinton said the water relief site was to help those without water. But in the interim another reason had clearly surfaced. "Now we've got a recent report showing that the Flint River water could have E. coli," McClinton told the council. "We're hearing from citizens about skin rashes, foul smells, and so on and so forth, so we're asking people to drop off water at Mission of Hope."

As the fall of 2014 set in, the water turned a chemical-looking blue. Or it did at Melissa Mays's house, on the south side of Flint, where the thirty-six-year-old mother looked at the water and laughed. "Oh, well, it smells like a swimming pool, it might as well look like one," she told her boys.

Melissa Mays, the mother of three boys, became an early and persistent advocate for a return to Great Lakes–sourced water.

Mays was a mother of three boys and had long brown hair, pale skin, and a sleeve of tattoos on one arm. She worked part-time in public relations for heavy metal bands and some called her the "metal lady." Over time the name would stick, but the meaning would change completely. Mays called city hall about the blue water and was told not to worry—just hard water and old pipes. "Phew," Mays said. "We can't afford to have our pipes replaced now but we're going to be OK."

Then Mays's cat started vomiting. Mays stroked the cat, and cat hair came out in her hand. Her three boys had already developed painful, untreatable rashes, and now their hair turned from silky to wiry. Soon Mays fell ill. When she got an upper respiratory infection, she coughed up a taste of cleaning fluid. The whole family, meanwhile, complained of achy bones. One son fell off a bike and broke his wrist in two places. Later the houseplants died.

Mays began to tune in to the day-to-day news about water. In September Flint issued two more boil water advisories due to bacteria found in feces; engineers added more chlorine at the water plant. Water shutoffs continued, as did citizen complaints. In October, Jan Burgess, who is legally blind, wrote to the US Environmental Protection Agency. She said her water had tripled in cost and yet smelled like pond scum. "It often is brown in color and frequently has particles floating in it," she wrote. Burgess noted the boil water advisories. "The water is not safe to drink, cook, or wash dishes with. Or even give to pets. We worry every time we shower."

Officials said the water was fine. Then again in mid-October, they appeared to acknowledge that it wasn't.

General Motors still operated three plants in Flint, and the

carmaker had complained within days of the switchover that engine crankshafts showed rust after they were machined with the newly sourced river water. Paint was peeling off auto body parts. The car company tried diluting the new river water with trucked-in water at substantial cost. When that didn't work, GM went back to Flint officials. They needed to return to Detroit water as soon as possible. Flint officials agreed. On October 13, GM announced that it would reconnect with Detroit-treated Lake Huron water for use in its engine factory.

Losing GM as a water customer meant Flint was out $400,000 a year, which residents would have to absorb. But worse, why had Emergency Manager Earley cut a deal with GM to get its factory off the river water while ignoring Flint residents' concerns? Now state officials seemed to thread a needle: the water was bad for metal but not for people. Mike Prysby, a state water engineer, shared with colleagues what he had told a *Flint Journal* reporter: "I stressed the importance of not branding Flint's water as 'corrosive' from a public health standpoint simply because it does not meet a manufacturing facility's limit for production."

That claim landed as an absurdity in Flint, where the move elicited the most forceful and angry round of protest yet, though no national attention. In a round of letters to the *Flint Journal*, the public raised rational though alarmed questions. "Apparently the city of Flint's water quality is not good enough to be used in an industrial process but good enough to [be] used and consumed by humans," wrote Flint resident D'Andre Jackson. "That the water can be corrosive to metal has me questioning whether or not the water is truly safe for me and my family and this community. It's hard to imagine that this would be allowed to happen anywhere else but within a city like Flint that most politicians would like to write off and forget about."

At a November city council meeting the same questions surfaced. Carolyn Shannon, a Flint elder with short-cropped hair, walked slowly toward the microphone. A frequent speaker, Shannon was soft-spoken and wore gloves. She had served food in the executive dining room of the once-elegant Durant hotel, waiting on auto tycoons. Her unfailing politeness gave weight to her grievance. "Good evening, Mr. President, and congratulations," she said to the newly appointed Josh Freeman.

Then her tone shifted slightly: "About this water. We do not know the long-term effects on our physical being," said Shannon, adding that her skin was scaly. "I can't drink it, I can't cook with it. So I'm spending a lot of money on bottled water, just water in my family.

"So I'm asking you to move away from this water like GM. If it corrodes General Motors metal parts, what do you think it will corrode on the inside of our bodies?"

≋

If the GM move didn't prompt attention, another alert soon would. On January 2, 2015, Melissa Mays was sorting through her mail. One folded-up item from the City of Flint looked unimportant and Mays aimed it toward the trash. She was already upset about the December water bill she had just paid for $532. She couldn't bear to look again. "I don't care," she said to herself.

Then she opened it.

The words, in tiny print, were unpronounceable. Mays studied the text until she began to understand. Flint water was in violation of a law—the federal Safe Water Drinking Act. To kill off the high levels of E. coli bacteria over the summer, the water plant had aggressively disinfected Flint River water with chlorine. But too much chlorine, when mixed with organic material like dead leaves, produced elevated total trihalomethanes, or TTHMs, chemical byproducts that can lead to liver, kidney, or neurological disorders, and even cancer. Not right away, but over time.

The high TTHM count had first surfaced about eight months earlier. But federal regulations required public notice only after the count was high over a series of months. And the violation posed no immediate health risk—except among the very young, very old, or immunocompromised, the notice said. In that case, a person should talk to their doctor.

Flint officials said the water was safe. "My family and I drink it and use it every day," Mayor Walling told a radio reporter.

Mays stared at the letter. The city had known for eight months of high TTHM levels and said nothing. That fact rankled, even if the city had acted within the law on notification. How could she believe what they were telling her if this information had been withheld from the public during all this time? Mays googled "total trihalomethanes" and found more information that described harms well beyond what the letter described. The TTHM law itself was decades old and had not kept pace with science. "Oh hell no," Mays said to herself. She stayed up all night gathering data and then turned to Facebook. She discovered that a friend from her music life was organizing a protest at city hall. That made Mays nervous. People who protested always looked half crazy on the news.

She called Erin Brockovich, the environmental activist who

had discovered poisoned water in Hinkley, California. Then Mays jumped into the public fray. She started attending council meetings, where she heard stories of pets dying, kidneys failing, seniors suffering, tomatoes withering and turning black on the vine. She met Shariff and Jefferson. She met another mom-activist and the two became fast partners. They formed the organization Water You Fighting For? and created a Facebook group, soon attracting thousands of members. Mays, too, had become a water warrior.

LeeAnne Walters (wearing 54) and her daughter, Kaylie, invite a state-appointed official to look closely at two water samples taken from their taps following a raucous meeting at Flint City Hall. The January 2015 meeting was among the first to bring residents together to advocate for safe water.

4

To the Dome

LeeAnne Walters did not necessarily broadcast that she and her husband had suffered the loss of a stillborn child. Maybe that's what made them so ferociously protective of their four other children. Walters was no shy thing. She valued her gut instinct and brazen honesty. One of her T-shirts read "Blood, Sweat, Respect." For a time, the top of her Facebook page asserted that "a worried mother does research better than the FBI."

Walters was a stay-at-home mother with flowing brown hair, a light-toned complexion, and a throaty, direct manner of speaking. She was married to a navy man, and they believed the water their family used was clean and safe. After all, before they moved into their two-story masonry home on the south side of Flint, the pipes had been stolen by vandals looking to sell the metal as scrap. The Walterses had then installed new plastic plumbing and a whole-house water filter.

During the summer of 2014, though, skin rashes erupted in the Walters household. Kaylie, a senior in high school, discovered red bumps on her fingers and toes and under her breasts. Son JD, who was fourteen, had a rash and so did Walters's three-year-old twins, Garrett and Gavin. One day Walters filled an inflatable pool in the backyard and let Gavin wade around in the water. He emerged covered in red splotches. And when the family celebrated Kaylie's graduation with an open house and pool party in August, those who swam came out of the water with more red spots on their skin. Doctors diagnosed scabies, eczema, dermatitis. It was all strange and puzzling. The diagnoses changed, but the skin eruptions refused to go away.

One fall day Kaylie was showering, shampooing her thick, dark hair, the glorious mane that looked just like a pony's tail when she gathered it in a hair tie. She applied conditioner, letting it sit for a minute or two before she began to rinse it out. She loved her hair. She ran her fingers through it and pulled her hand away, gripping a massive clump of hair. It was gruesome and frightening. "Mom, Mom, come here," she screamed.

LeeAnne Walters came running. She looked at the wad of hair in her daughter's hand. "What did you do?" she asked with alarm.

"Nothing," Kaylie cried. "I was just conditioning and it came out."

Not long after, Walters's longtime hairdresser noticed that LeeAnne's lustrous long hair was thinning in patches. Then her eyelashes disappeared. She began wearing fake ones to hide the loss. Walters didn't know that elsewhere in Flint people were going through the same hair loss and were also wondering why.

Meanwhile, the preschool-aged Walters twins had started to

complain about aches and pains. Gavin, who had a compromised immune system, stopped growing. He also had trouble pronouncing some words that his mom knew he had never struggled with before. And in November, her older son, JD, had a bout of abdominal pain so severe that he wound up in the hospital and missed a month of school. Doctors puzzled over the cause.

In late December, Walters and her husband, Dennis, were loading the dishwasher when LeeAnne turned on the tap and watched a stream of orange-brown water spill out. "What's going on here?" she called out.

Walters contacted the City of Flint. They were "winterizing the system," she was told. Nothing to worry about. But Walters noticed something else: the whole-house filter that trapped particulates and had needed replacing every six months now required a change every week or two. She later learned that the filter was meant to eliminate sediment only. It wouldn't capture anything dissolved in the water.

A few days later, on January 2, Walters received the same water violation notice in the mail that Melissa Mays had read: the one about the federal drinking water law and the mysterious TTHMs. It warned against anyone drinking the water who had a compromised immune system—like Gavin, one of Walters's twin boys. His doctor told Walters they needed to drink bottled water. The brown-water bouts continued. The couple was baffled. LeeAnne, who had a degree as a medical assistant, began doing research. She and Dennis started going to council meetings, which is where she first learned that she wasn't alone.

≈≈≈

The arctic weather on the evening of January 13, 2015, failed to deter some two hundred hearty Flint residents who gathered at a vast banquet hall at the Antioch Missionary Baptist Church. An overflowing crowd in puffy jackets leaned against walls. Two boys held homemade signs: "flint water good for sh . . ." said one in block letters.

The mayor and council sat facing the crowd across the front of the room. Soon the standing microphone went to citizens.

Gladyes Williamson, a sixty-year-old woman with long white-blond hair, held up a jug full of a pale almond-colored liquid that would become a regular feature of water protests. It was her tap water from August, and it had ruined her brand-new water pump and wreaked havoc in her life, she told the crowd. Quiana Dawson said her two young children were breaking out in rashes from bathing in the water, and her doctor bills were mounting. LeeAnne Walters similarly described her three-year-olds' skin problems after bathing. Tom Herman, seventy-five and bearded, said he was "very suspicious" of the river water. The city had said residents would notice little change. Now, if you were old, you were warned to talk to your doctor. "I'd like to get a little older," Herman said.

In the cold days that followed, other Flint residents said their trust in government was withering away. A group of sixteen people from the city's Ward Seven, an area with the highest rates of advanced degrees and the lowest in poverty, wrote a letter to City Hall saying water problems had "undermined our confidence" in people at the top. Other complaints rained on state legislators and state agencies. In summary, one state official said, the calls added up to "a significant (I think they used the word complete) loss of public confidence in the drinking water quality in Flint."

As the public grew more suspicious of their water, state and local officials scrambled to bolster their claims of water safety. They called the first in a series of town hall meetings where they would bring in officials to face residents directly. "We want the residents, businesses, and visitors of Flint to know that the water in Flint is safe," said a city hall press release. The goal was to reassure the public that Flint was "on the right track." Experts hired by the city would be on hand to answer written questions at the end of the meeting.

On January 21, a protest took place outside of Flint City Hall. The crowd was raw with anger, one report said. People were in an uproar, said Councilman Mays. Protesters carried homemade signs: "Are You Trying To Kill Us?"

A few hours later, the protesters joined a larger gathering in an auditorium known as the "Dome," an add-on to city hall that looked as if a dilapidated spaceship had landed on the complex. People who had never attended a meeting before weathered the unplowed streets to go to the Dome. They were young and old, black and white, wealthy and poor, educated and not. A restlessness pervaded the room. The overflowing crowd spilled out into the hallway.

The meeting would be run by Howard Croft, the director of Flint's Department of Public Works. Croft was responsible for parks and recreation, street maintenance, water and sewer, garbage collection, the planning department, fleet management, and economic development. Previously, he had run a solar panel company. On paper, at least, he had no special knowledge in water treatment or engineering. On this night the police chief and several uniformed officers roamed the Dome. Croft told the crowd, "If there is a disruption, the police are prepared [to end the meeting]."

≋

Walters, with husband Dennis and daughter Kaylie, brought two bottles of filtered tap water labeled by date, time, and place. She had captured one sample just before leaving the house. The three walked into the small leaky auditorium. Soon residents were asked to submit questions in writing to be read aloud and answered at the end. Walters submitted hers and waited.

The presentation began with a PowerPoint explaining the chemical structure of disinfection byproducts, followed by a chart of every test site reading in Flint over the past months. Residents sighed. This felt like a lecture, not a meeting to answer citizen concerns. Many residents, thanks to the internet, had already schooled themselves about TTHMs. They didn't need a lecture; they had questions.

Like Walters, many had brought bottles, jars, and jugs of discolored tap water, like an array of flavors in shades of mud brown, rusty red-orange, pale green, or yellow, some with bits of sand or metal floating at the bottom. A resident brought a handful of his own white hair—lost, he believed, to toxic water. The evidence seemed at odds with the assurances from the panel. Some of those sounded like riddles: "Is there a risk in the short term? That depends on you," said Stephen Busch, a dough-faced, prematurely white-haired official with the Michigan Department of Environmental Quality. "It's an individual thing. You can make a judgment [after talking to your doctor]."

Busch had registered concern about using the Flint River less than a year earlier, when he wrote in a memo to colleagues that river water could cause public health problems due to "microbial risks" and required more use of chlorine to disinfect, which could lead to more public exposure to cancer-causing chemicals. The river would also require more regulation and plant upgrades than lake water, he wrote.

Now Busch was defending the river while the meeting turned to chaos. People shouted. One woman reportedly pulled down a part of her pants to expose a rash on her buttocks.

Gladyes Williamson was back with her jug of urine-colored water, lifted again into the air.

"Will you drink this?" she asked.

"I'm not going to drink that water," a panelist said.

"Then why are we here?"

Councilman Mays tried to keep the peace: "Just be cool a minute," he said in his deep voice.

A microbiologist from Michigan State University, Joan Rose, said the public would need to be patient while the distribution system was fixed. "Hang in there," she said. Another panelist said Flint could look forward to a return to Lake Huron water in about another year, or as soon as the pipeline was complete, to which a resident shouted, out of order: "What do we do until then?"

Croft warned that he would end the meeting if people didn't settle down.

Some ended it themselves, by walking out. Finally Croft shut it down.

≈≈≈

Walters didn't feel that her question had been answered in full. As people left, she approached the new emergency manager, Gerald

Ambrose, who had recently been appointed to replace Darnell Earley. Ambrose was Flint's fourth, after spending three years as Flint's director of finance.

Walters held up her two bottles of water with thumb and forefinger, as if dangling two dead mice by the tails. "Look, this is what's coming out of our tap," she told Ambrose. "We just collected this before we left."

Their color was not unlike the water samples of others in the room.

"There's no way that water came out of your tap," Ambrose told Walters. She must've added something to the water to turn it brown. He accused her of lying, of faking the water samples. She was stupid if she believed that was real Flint water. Flint water, he said, was safe to drink.

Walters's daughter, Kaylie, stood behind her mother, grimacing and feeling she might like to disappear. "Oooh, I'm getting out of swing range," she said to herself, taking a step back. She turned to a woman to her left. "I'm going to need to get bail money for my mom tonight because she's going to hit someone," she told her. Her mother was a "Jersey girl" who stood up to people.

Indeed, Walters had begun to churn. She was worried about her children. The city had led her to believe she was the sole person in Flint with a water problem. The recent meetings and protest had made clear that she was one among many. And now this man was publicly calling her a liar. With others crowded around, Walters felt humiliation turn to fury.

She held the bottles a little closer to the white-haired official. "This came out of my kitchen tap today and you better believe me because I'm not lying and I'm not stupid," she told Ambrose.

In the car on the way home, the family replayed the drama. Dennis Walters, who worked in law enforcement for the navy, offered the perspective of a detective. "There was all this physical evidence," he said. The water jugs, the rashes, the clumps of hair. "How do we make them hear us?"

Walters, with her medical background, said: "It looks like we've got to get to the science, because you can't argue with science."

Other residents described the Dome meeting as pandemonium, a textbook example of how never to run a meeting. It appeared to have increased public suspicion, not lessened it. A few days later at the regular January city council meeting, where the number of public speakers had grown lengthy, resident Keith Pemberton summarized what had happened at the Dome. When people first walked in, "We all had issues, we had problems, all individual stuff," he said.

As people left, "Everybody walked out of that meeting on the same team. After that meeting, we're one group."

During the 1920s, the US lead industry promoted the sale of paint by appealing to children. A coloring book created by the National Lead Company, producer of Dutch Boy Paint, told a story of children getting rid of Old Man Gloom by painting every inch of their house a cheerful, lead-based paint color.

5

Big Worries Here

Gavin was nearly four, and he wasn't growing as fast as his twin brother. He weighed thirty-two pounds compared to his brother's thirty-seven. It worried LeeAnne Walters. Her doctors said twins were generally smaller than most kids. "Yeah, but not my twins," Walters said.

After the disastrous January town hall meeting, Walters had begun staying up nights online, educating herself about water infrastructure and what can go wrong. At home the water stayed brown and Gavin's skin rashes worsened. Walters made a video of the "before" and "after" of Gavin's bathing, with the "after" showing big red blotches on his skin. Gavin's baths had become painful, shrieking events. Afterward Walters would try to soothe his skin with lotion, but Gavin screamed some more. She took the video to her doctor.

Walters had already signed up to have her water tested. "Yeah, yeah, get on the list," she was told. The next time she took Gavin to the doctor he wrote a note that the boy's skin reactions were likely due to water exposure. Walters took the note to city hall. "I became priority number one," she said.

The Walters family gathers in their living room while LeeAnne checks son Gavin for skin rashes after bathing. Gavin's growth was stunted during the water crisis, and he was found to suffer from lead poisoning and anemia, a common symptom of lead exposure.

A Flint water official visited the Walters home in February 2015. He inspected all the plumbing, saw black oily sediment in the toilet, and collected samples. About a week later he called back. The iron levels exceeded his instrument's highest measurements. He recommended another test. Two weeks later Walters received a voice mail, this one frantic: "Please," said the city water official, Mike Glasgow, "whatever you do, don't let your kids drink the water."

The next day Walters met with the official to go over test results. The problem was lead, he said, and his instructions were radical: Do not drink the water or mix it with juice. Do not cook with the water or bathe in it. The lead in the water had measured 104 parts per billion (ppb); Walters had no idea what the number meant. The official explained that the federal water standard is no greater than 15 ppb, and hers was seven times higher. He said he had never seen a number that high. In March, the measurement would shoot up to nearly 400 ppb.

Walters began going door to door in her neighborhood, warning friends and strangers about lead in the water. Some called her crazy.

≈≈≈

The high lead numbers in the water made Walters wonder whether lead was also coursing through the veins of her children. She wanted to get Gavin's blood tested especially, given his more vulnerable condition. Blood lead testing is required of one- and two-year-olds on Medicaid, the government insurance program that covers families unable to afford private insurance. But Walters's doctor asked for paperwork from the city before performing the test. The same day Walters picked up the paperwork and returned for the test. It showed Gavin's blood lead level was fine, the doctor told her, but he would not reveal the precise number. Walters later learned that her doctor was married to a staff person in the Flint emergency manager's office. She wondered whether that might have been a conflict.

Just in case, Walters found another doctor to perform another blood test, this one outside of Flint. A week later she received a call. She took the call in her kitchen toward the back of her home, and it was one of those surreal moments when time slows down. Gavin's blood lead level was 6.5 micrograms per deciliter (the measurement for lead in blood is expressed in micrograms per deciliter). The legal limit was 5 micrograms. The safe limit was 0, research showed. Gavin had lead poisoning and severe anemia, which was another of lead's ill effects.

Walters wrote down the results, and the numbers swam in front of her as she teared up. She would later say she had a nervous breakdown in her kitchen. But she also pulled herself together. Distraught, she gathered her paperwork and Gavin's blood results and drove herself to city hall. She went to the mayor's office, where she was sent to the city attorney's office. There they made copies of her paperwork, handed her a damage claim form, and instructed her to fill it out and include a dollar figure on the page, an amount Walters felt would compensate her for lead damage to Gavin. She could write down one million dollars if she wanted.

Walters looked up. "How the hell do I put a price tag on my child's life?" she asked. In the accumulating moments, this would be one more when she felt like punching someone.

In this telling, in the living room of her Flint home on a February day in 2019 during a heavy snowstorm, Walters is interrupted by Gavin, her lead-poisoned son. He races up and down the stairs as he and his twin brother build a snowman outside that they've named Jerry, after their uncle. "I'm going to grab one more rock and then four more rocks and then two more rocks," Gavin calls out as he whips through the living room.

His mother stops him, takes both of his thin shoulders and looks into his eyes. He has mispronounced all of his *r*'s. His rocks sound like "woks."

"Hey, look at me," she kindly instructs him. "Pronounce your *r*'s. Rrrrrrr. Rrrock."

"Rrrrrock," says Gavin.

"Very good."

≈≈≈

Once she received news of Gavin's poisoning in early 2015, Walters turned her investigative eye to lead, one of the oldest and best-known toxins in the world, dating back to ancient Rome, where it was first used in plumbing. Romans of the upper classes ate their meals from lead-based plates and drank from lead-based goblets—often sipping wine preserved with lead. It was a lead-laced world, and in later eras, lead was thought to cause everything from still-births to anemia and brain damage. Archaeologists once theorized that lead poisoning contributed to the fall of the Roman Empire. More recent science had cast doubt on the theory.

In eighteenth-century England, though, doctors discovered a strange illness arising every year among residents of counties that produced apple cider. Each season those involved in production showed signs of what became known as the Devonshire colic, described in gruesome detail by one local doctor, John Huxham:

> This disease began its attack by an excessively tormenting pain in the stomach [. . .] with an unequal weak pulse, and coldish sweats; the tongue in the meantime was coated with a greenish, or brown, mucus, and the breath was most offensive. An

> enormous vomiting soon followed, for the most part
> of exceeding green bile, sometimes black, with a
> great quantity of phlegm excessively acid and very
> tough; nay the foul matter brought up was oftentimes
> so very acrid, that, by excoriating the throat and the
> oesophagus, it was tinged with blood, and created a
> difficulty and pain in swallowing.

Only later did doctors make the connection between Devonshire colic and lead poisoning—from the cider-making presses and the holding tanks and drinking vessels lined with lead.

Lead poisoning increased during the industrial age, and its recognized symptoms included joint and muscle pain, kidney failure, hypertension, and episodes of "lead gout," described by one researcher as "sharp onset and recurrent spasms, in which the patient writhes in pain, retracts his legs spasmodically to his abdomen, groans, clenches his hands, grits his teeth, with beads of sweat on his brow." In the most severe cases it resulted in blindness and death.

As the hazards of lead became better known during the twentieth century, the American lead industry fought back with ad campaigns targeting children. The National Lead Company, for example, used a cartoon character, Dutch Boy, in its advertising. Makers of lead paint blamed poor and nonwhite people for the poisoning. The problem was the residents of "slum dwellings"—who were "relatively ignorant" and "ineducable," and whose children ate the sweet-tasting lead paint, according to internal Lead Industries Association documents.

By the 1970s, a Philadelphia researcher, Dr. Herbert Needleman, learned by testing hundreds of baby teeth that lead was present in children of every race and social class. With that discovery came the attention of the US government. Lead paint was banned in 1978 and lead in gasoline was completely prohibited by 1995. Lead exposure, however, remained widespread, since it existed in the paint of old homes, in the air and soil, and in the water that circulated through lead pipes.

Today, research shows that lead even at the lowest levels can be highly destructive. It acts as a kind of impostor, tricking the body into receiving it like calcium. Lead replaces calcium in the bones, in the red blood cells that carry oxygen throughout the body, and in the pathways of the brain, jamming the neurons that allow the brain to function.

That's what LeeAnne Walters learned: there is no safe level of lead exposure, and the younger the child the more harmful lead can be. From the moment of a child's conception, lead can interfere with the rapid, extremely delicate, and highly complex development of the human brain. This is why lead can cause brain damage and lowered IQ. It can trigger anemia, hearing loss, slowed growth, and reduced nerve function. It has been linked to aggressive behavior and violent crime. Lead exposure in even small amounts can reprogram genes and contribute to a greater risk of disease later in life. The genetic scrambling may be passed along to the next generation.

There is no way of reversing the damage done by lead, though a diet high in calcium, iron, and vitamin C can help the body absorb less of it, Walters learned.

And adults are hardly immune. Their fully developed brains and bodies may be less vulnerable, yet studies link lead exposure in adults to kidney disease, increased blood pressure, and stroke. In seniors, lead exposure can worsen dementia. In pregnant women, it has been linked to stillbirth and low birth weights.

≈≈≈

Walters schooled herself in the horrors of lead while officials insisted her lead-laced water was unique to her home. The city's immediate solution was to attach four garden hoses end-to-end to hook up to a neighbor's spigot. Walters and her family could use that water for showers and the laundry but not to drink. The hoses would have to do until the ground thawed and the city could replace the 150-foot lead service line to the house.

Dissatisfied, Walters scoured the internet for help. She came across the name of someone at the Environmental Protection Agency in Chicago, the federal agency tasked as watchdog of Michigan waters. His name was Miguel Del Toral, and he was an expert on lead in public water systems. Walters called Del Toral and told him about everything, from her family's brown water to her lead test results to Gavin's poisoning.

The call raised immediate concern at the EPA, at least with Miguel Del Toral. He circulated Walters's information to colleagues, and one of them soon contacted drinking water regulators in Michigan. "The main purpose of my email," the EPA official wrote to Michigan water officials at the Department of Environmental Quality, "is to alert you to the high lead levels reported to a citizen yesterday by Flint Water Dept." She described the sediments, brown water, rashes, and hair loss at the Walters home. And she relayed the lead test results with a startled, "WOW!!!! Did he find the LEAD! 104 ppb. She has two children under the age of three. . . . Big worries here."

The Chicago official, Jennifer Crooks, went on to speculate about what was going wrong. She worried that "different chemistry water is leaching out contaminants from the insides of [. . .] the pipes."

State officials deflected the concerns presented by the EPA's Crooks. More than 20,000 email messages related to Flint's bad water would zip among city, county, state, and federal offices, creating a years-long digital trail of damning and scornful notes later made public. In this exchange, Michigan officials reassured Crooks, saying there was no cause for alarm. Flint water met all regulatory standards. It was just the Walters home, which was already on their radar. The state would do more work there by retesting, flushing taps, and "providing lead reduction strategies to Mrs. Walters."

Walters continued her conversations with the EPA's Del Toral while Michigan water official Stephen Busch complained to colleagues that the EPA was meddling: "Not sure why [the EPA Chicago office] sees this one sample as such a big deal," he wrote.

Meanwhile, as the crisis progressed, state officials spoke ill of Walters and dismissed her concerns. In their view she was a "very vocal resident" who was "raising hell with the locals." She became one among "a steady parade of community groups keeping everyone hopped-up and misinformed." Later, during a phone call with a nurse from the Michigan Department of Health and Human Services, Walters described her worries about Gavin's lead poisoning. "It's just a few IQ points," the nurse said, according to Walters. "It's not the end of the world."

Top: Ariana Hawk helps her children get ready for preschool by brushing their teeth with bottled water four years after the crisis began, in April 2018. *Bottom*: Journey Jones, three, sits on the kitchen floor in her family's home as her brother Iveon, two, reaches for a bottle of water. The two are among six siblings who have tested positive for elevated lead in their blood.

6

Ten Thousand Children

The so-called big worries by an EPA higher-up in Chicago, expressed to careless water guardians in Lansing, failed completely to trickle down to parents, infants, children, and youth in Flint. Yet Flint's youngest children resided at the epicenter. Some 10,000 Flint children under the age of six took the brunt of befouled Flint water, it was later estimated. Their growing bones and brains absorbed more lead than any other age group. Flint's youngest served like soldiers on the front lines of a war and faced the enemy: contaminated water and its enablers.

All over the city, children of every age showed signs of physical harm or psychological trauma. Water tainted with bacteria or heavy metals, in children's imaginative leaps, became liquid kryptonite or Ebola, the rare and deadly virus, spurting from every school drinking fountain. Soni Sparks taught in an elementary school in Beecher near the Flint border, drawing Flint students. Her charges had come to believe water fountains on the southern Flint side of the school gushed poison. They went running to the northern Beecher side to use the fountains there. Teachers tried to explain.

Teachers and parents alike nurtured a new anguish: in a city already stigmatized as failing, Flint children would internalize a

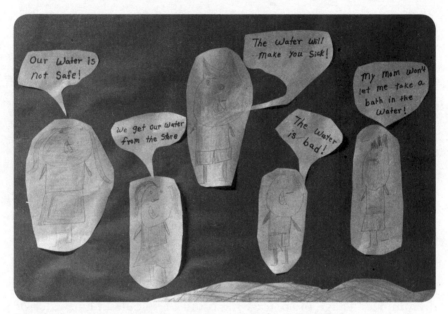

A preschool art project reveals how Flint's youngest residents fear their water. "The water will make you sick," says one. "My mom won't let me take a bath in the water," says another.

message that Flint water would mark them for life. Many had asked whether they would die from the water, or whether it could make them "dumb." Some seemed to believe the latter—or leaned on bad water as a handy new dog-ate-my-homework excuse. "I can't do this, I drank lead in my water," a struggling student complained to Sparks in an after-school literacy program she helps operate on Flint's north side.

Sparks had no way of knowing the truth, but it wasn't the first time she'd heard the line. "Let's try again and see," she told the child. "Let's beat this. Don't let it conquer you. You conquer it."

Over time, all ages learned to shy away from tap water, with its scary power to harm. During a radio show broadcast about the crisis, held at the Flint Institute of Arts, a ten-year-old girl, Meredith, said the water made her fear for her future. "I take school really seriously," she said. "I want to become smart. And I'm afraid this is gonna make me not become . . . like, not let me be my fullest self."

Kent Key, Director of the Office of Community Scholars and Partnerships at Michigan State University College of Human Medicine, believed negative water messages could harm Flint youth. Flint kids were not "victims" and should not jump to worst-case stories of lead poisoning like lowered IQ or violent behavior. He wanted to "saturate the city" with positive messaging for youth: Flint kids are smart.

Flint kids proved plenty smart enough to absorb their parents' earliest suspicions about water. Bishop Jefferson, the activist pastor and early water warrior, warned her children and grandchildren not to use water fountains at school. Montae Cherry, one of the bishop's grandsons, knew what to do when his third-grade class lined up after recess: he detoured from the water fountain line to the restroom. Many children internalized the threat of tap water. They'd do anything to avoid drinking that gruesome, fetid, poop-scented brew.

Newborns were extremely vulnerable, especially when young mothers used tap water to mix formula. New mom Erika Thompson complained to the city council on behalf of her four-month-old son back in June of 2014. Every day the boy's grandmother put his baby bottle in a warming device. Over a period of weeks a residue had collected in the warmer. "It was as if an ashtray had been dumped in my child's bottle warmer," Thompson said, incredulous, "where he's fed."

Ariana Hawk was twenty-four, pregnant, and the mother of two when the water was switched. She thought drinking river water was a bad idea but paid it little mind. In late 2014 Hawk gave birth to a daughter who stopped breathing at home. An ambulance took her baby to the hospital where she was diagnosed with pneumonia and survived after a two-week stay. Soon after, her daughter's father developed a bacterial pneumonia. He died at age forty-one.

〜〜〜

While some exaggerated, many other children and youth did not know or did not heed warnings about water. "I just kept drinking it," reflected Delante Mckenney, who was in middle school when the water was switched. "I was thirsty. I thought all water was good. Who would be concerned with drinking water out of the faucet?"

He stopped when the water turned brown.

In the early months after the switch to the river, Mckenney's younger half brother developed leg pains. "He was extra skinny," said Mckenney. "He was small for his age. He's still skinny." The younger boy tested positive for lead poisoning.

Mckenney's friend, A'Tyries Belin, didn't know whether he had been exposed to toxins or not. His mother, a health care worker, sent him to a doctor, who told him he was low on calcium. He took calcium pills. He hated taking pills.

〜〜〜

Ny'Azia Johnson was in early high school when she and her family established a new water routine in response to rumors. Her grandmother and mother awoke before dawn each weekday morning to heat pots of bottled water on the kitchen stove. By the time Johnson awoke around 5:30 a.m., a pot of heated water awaited. Johnson poured her water into a sink basin or tub, or dipped from the pot to take a sponge bath. She couldn't wash her hair alone. How do you rinse soap from hair with bottled water? It never felt clean.

Johnson was an excellent student with lots of extracurriculars. She got tired of the water drill. She got lazy. It was too much work. And anyway, after the January uproar and media reports, the news and talk about Flint's water died down. The press had mostly

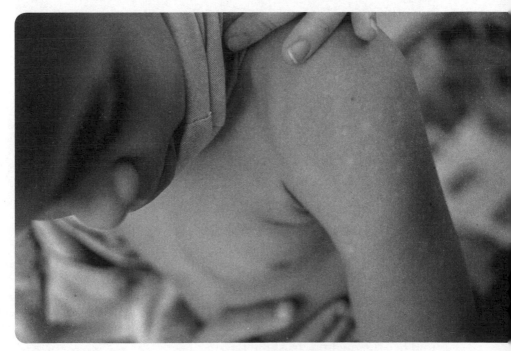

Twelve-year-old Jeremiah Loren bathed in Flint River water during the crisis before his parents knew of its ill effects. They noticed rashes across their son's arms, neck, and back in January 2016.

disappeared. From her point of view that meant the water was probably fine. She certainly wanted it to be fine. She switched to tap. It
was far easier.

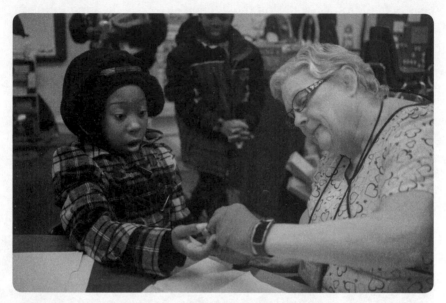

Ti' Nisha Norman has her blood lead levels tested at Freeman Elementary School's Family Fun and
Lead Testing night in January 2016.

That's when Johnson's skin began to break out in rashes of red,
rough, painful bumps all over her face and neck. She didn't connect
the rash to tap water at first. She stared at the outbreak in the mir-
ror. She tried scrubbing the bumps, lancing them, using acne medication. Finally she wondered whether a switch back to her bottled
water routine might help. Within two weeks of switching the rash
calmed down, except for the black-and-brown scars that remained.
She stuck with the onerous routine of washing with bottled.

Johnson didn't trust the tap. And she didn't trust the people who
told her she ought to trust the tap.

And that was probably wise. Five and half years later, state data would show that one in five public school children in Flint was eligible for special education, an increase of 56 percent since before the water crisis began, according to state figures. No one could pin the increase precisely on lead exposure. But by then everyone knew that Flint children had been exposed for many months, and that any amount of lead exposure can hurt a child's brain.

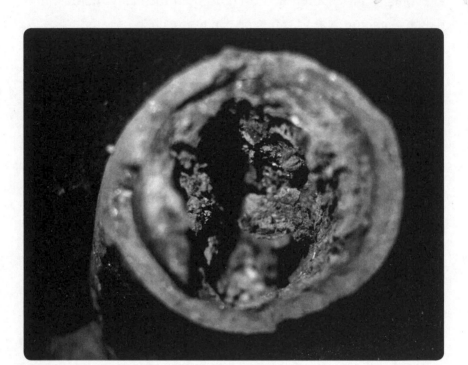

One of the first lead pipes removed from Veronica Kelly's home on Flint's north side shows corrosion after the city's switch to highly acidic Flint River water.

7

A Good Guess

A colleague once swore to a congressional committee that Miguel Del Toral knew more than anybody in the world about lead in water. But Del Toral didn't flaunt it. When the water expert spoke, his style was measured and humble. He wore a short-cropped salt-and-pepper beard and glasses. Later, when he arrived on the scene in Flint, his T-shirt revealed a self-mocking wit: "In My Defense, I Was Left Unsupervised."

With his calm expertise, from his office in Chicago, Del Toral mentored LeeAnne Walters throughout 2015. He explained in plain English the odyssey of turning raw water into drinking water. He knew water drawn from a river might encounter a thousand pollutants en route: road salts, fertilizers, animal waste, toxic chemicals, or countless others.

At a treatment plant, water was processed for drinking. From the plant it whooshed into a city's underground water distribution system, where it could react with metals in untold variations.

The more Del Toral learned about Flint, the more he doubted its drinking water was safe. First he questioned the testing methods. Government testers in Michigan ran a tap, or "flushed" it, for at least five minutes before capturing a sample. They also flushed fire hydrants all over the city. This method would dilute the amount of lead and other contaminants in any sample and result in misleadingly low readings. Del Toral feared skewed test results might give Flint residents a false sense of security. He guessed that all of Flint might be drinking lead.

Del Toral was already skeptical about switching the city's water from one of the Great Lakes to the Flint River. Lake Huron's water intake was a half mile offshore, where the water was deep, cold, fresh, clear, and more constant in flow and temperature.

The relatively shallow Flint River, on the other hand, ebbed and rose day to day, its volume increasing and falling with heavy rain or summer drought. That meant concentrations changed and temperatures fluctuated. The Flint River had many more warm days out of a year than Lake Huron, making it more hospitable to dangerous bacteria.

And the river had a grotesque toxic history. Industry through the ages, and especially General Motors, had used the Flint River as the collective dumping ground for chemical disposal and sludge. GM's suppliers upriver of Flint also contributed to the mix. Fish kills, or localized die-offs, had once plagued the river. As early as 1933, a conservation officer sent seven fish on ice to the University of Michigan for testing. The analysis showed that pollution had robbed the water of oxygen; the fish had suffocated. Slicked with oil and other flammables, the river was said to have caught fire twice. That's why in 1964 Flint switched from the river to Great Lakes water. Since then, no engineer had ever recommended the river as a full-time water source. Many had advised against it.

Overwhelmingly, as the possibility arose, residents recoiled at the thought. The river loomed in Flint's collective imagination as a freakish no-man's land of shopping carts, junked cars, and decomposed bodies. "You want some water with your dead bodies?" Township classmates of Walters's daughter, Kaylie, disparaged the river when first learning of the switch. Indeed, after the 2014 switch, tow trucks and divers continued to hoist cars and pollutants from the bottom. It didn't stop some of the desperate or hungry from fishing from the river. But the state warned against eating too many walleye, bass, or catfish from the Flint because of chemicals toxic to humans, including mercury.

But to be fair, the river's image also required updating. It had undergone dramatic improvement after passage of the Clean Water Act of 1972, which regulated what could be dumped in the nation's waterways. In recent years the Flint River had attracted endangered wildlife and been rediscovered too by river keepers for recreation. They worked to further rebrand the river as an asset to the city, and annual cleanups drew passionate volunteers.

Still, no matter how it had revived, the river remained highly sensitive as a drinking water source. Hired experts had told Flint as much a decade earlier. Road salt runoff, especially, made the river highly corrosive, as it did for most northern rivers. Using the river for public drinking was possible, but it required a sophisticated understanding of water treatment and more elaborate equipment to proceed. In Flint, Del Toral did not detect either sophistication or a state-of-the-art plant.

And that was *before* the water slipped into Flint's ancient distribution system, some 600 miles of tubular underground byways built in the nineteenth century. The average age of a Flint water main is about eighty-three years, the same as for its 7,000 old valves, the levers used to redirect the water from one distribution area or neighborhood to another. Many of those were stuck in the on or off position.

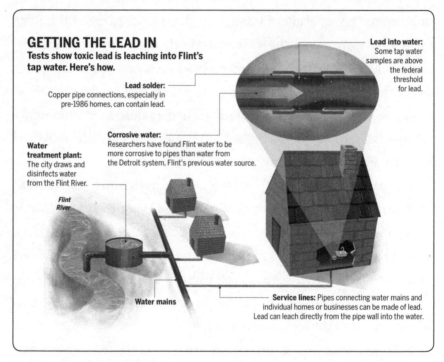

GETTING THE LEAD IN
Tests show toxic lead is leaching into Flint's tap water. Here's how.

Lead solder: Copper pipe connections, especially in pre-1986 homes, can contain lead.

Lead into water: Some tap water samples are above the federal threshold for lead.

Corrosive water: Researchers have found Flint water to be more corrosive to pipes than water from the Detroit system, Flint's previous water source.

Water treatment plant: The city draws and disinfects water from the Flint River.

Flint River

Water mains

Service lines: Pipes connecting water mains and individual homes or businesses can be made of lead. Lead can leach directly from the pipe wall into the water.

Flint River water was never treated appropriately at the plant for its corrosive properties. When it circulated through the city's underground system of pipes, the highly acidic water stripped away pipe interiors, whisking lead and deadly bacteria into houses for drinking, cooking, and bathing.

There was another challenge: the footprint of Flint's water system is too large for the ever-contracting population. Water stagnation in "dead ends" or "dead legs" of up to a month can occur in some spots, creating more hospitable breeding places for bacteria. And the system's uneven hydraulics, or the pumping of water through the unwieldy old pipes, works like sluggish blood circulating through clogged arteries. Adding chlorine disinfectant to the water on the east side doesn't necessarily ensure chlorine disinfection on the west side of town.

As flustered water engineers sought to move the water along, they flushed and flushed; fire hydrants spewed water all over Flint, forming brown rivers and eddies along streets and in ditches. Bacterial counts soared anyway, leading to the three boil water advisories in August and September 2014, the ones that had found excessive fecal coliform bacteria from human and animal waste. That was when Nayyirah Shariff had first begun boiling.

Back at the plant, Flint's water engineers added more chlorine, which was what had led to the TTHM violations, those excessive chemical byproducts that could cause cancer. That was no surprise. To water chemists, the spaghetti-like system of pipes underground acted like a very long chemical reactor. Things happened there—unseeable events. A droplet could leave a treatment plant as fresh as spring water, only to spill out of a kitchen faucet as toxic waste.

Del Toral knew that possibility was far more likely in old industrial Flint, where a local law passed in 1897 required all pipes to be made of lead. Now they had been banned. But America's oldest cities still relied on millions of miles of lead pipes for their water—pipes slowly deteriorating with age—and Flint was one of them.

There were treatment Band-Aids for the lead pipe problem. For more than fifty years Detroit had adhered to standard practice by treating water with phosphates, chemicals that reduced acidity. Reducing water acidity kept metal pipes—lead pipes—from corroding. Over time, the phosphates formed a protective coating, or "scale," on the inside of the pipes. The coating acted like an interior raincoat or liner—a barrier between the interior surface of the metal pipe and the water running through it. The phosphate treatment is known as corrosion control.

Without corrosion control, the pipes might rust out like car undersides after a long winter of salted roads. Without phosphates, corrosive water would shave away the pipes' interior scale. It would loosen metal bits, unleash unwanted bacteria, and offer all the nasty particles a free ride to the tap.

Del Toral pressed on with Michigan water officials. In emails, he and Crooks asked whether Flint was using corrosion control. The rust-colored water that Flint residents complained about suggested the pipes were being stripped of iron. And "'high levels of iron usually bring high levels of lead,'" wrote Crooks, quoting Del Toral.

Michigan officials once again blandly reassured the EPA. Flint was using optimized corrosion control, they said. But the vagueness of their answer failed to reassure.

Del Toral deployed LeeAnne Walters, the worried mother with the investigative nose. He was not receiving enough information directly from state officials. From his office in Chicago, he directed Walters on the ground in Flint. He knew what to look for; Walters found it. Soon she had her hands on the list of chemicals Flint was adding to its river water. Del Toral got a call. Walters began reading.

"What are you reading?" Del Toral asked.

She told him.

He asked her to read the list again.

And again.

"Okay, flip the page," Del Toral said.

There were only numbers on the next page, and the page after that.

"You've got to send that to me," Del Toral said.

Walters sent him the list.

Shortly after, Del Toral called back with alarm.

Something was missing, and the consequences could be grave.

Graffiti throughout Flint documents public anger about water, as in this rendering of children drinking and selling glasses of "Leadmonade." Photographed at Kearsley Park in September 2018.

8

Water Out of Control

Flint's bright-white water tower rose above the city like a sixteen-legged monument. At its feet lay the flat-roofed, sand-colored Flint Water Treatment Plant on the bank of the Flint River. When Flint activated the plant for its first full-time use in fifty years, the old machinery limped and groaned to a start. "It was sort of like Grandma's Chevy," said one water expert. "Full of spiders, dust, and bad oil."

The expert, Robert Bowcock, was an associate of Erin Brockovich, the environmental activist who had inspired the film by the same name. At the request of Flint activists, he visited Flint on a freezing February day in 2015 as a consultant to troubleshoot the city's water. "It was generally in disrepair," Bowcock later testified in court. "Just a dirty old treatment plant—not the kind of thing that you just whimsically fire up to save a few bucks."

When the mothballed plant creaked to life, it contained

broken-down equipment, an inadequate supply of chemicals, an untested setup, and an untrained and meager staff. In the preceding years, consultants had said upgrades to the plant could cost more than $60 million—or $100 million in today's dollars. Others had said $25 million. Flint was broke, so it scraped together $8 million for the job.

Predictably, repairs had been hasty and far from complete. Even someone from the distance of a desk chair in Lansing warned against it. The haste, said Brian Larkin, a staffer in the governor's Office of Urban Initiatives, "could lead to some big potential disasters down the road."

Plant employees felt uneasy, too. The water quality supervisor, Michael Glasgow, said he felt pressured and wasn't ready. A week before bringing the equipment back online, he wrote to higher-ups. "I do not anticipate giving the OK to begin sending water out anytime soon." He added: "If water is distributed from this plant in the next couple weeks, it will be against my direction."

Many agreed. A 2011 analysis of the river as a drinking water source, prepared for Mayor Walling, estimated that readying the plant, built in 1952, could take five years or more. A county official from the drain commission said the plant was three months from ready. A consultant hired by the city advised a two- to three-month test run, which was never done. A lab specialist said she and others were learning "on the fly" and needed six more weeks of training. Another drain commission official later said the plant was barely halfway through a multiyear renovation. And Glasgow didn't understand why there were only twenty-six employees at the plant now when there had been forty a decade earlier, back when the plant was used as merely a backup to water supplied by Detroit.

But pressures from above superseded safety or readiness. The state was not willing to listen, to wait, to make sure the plant and staff were ready. A breakneck schedule mattered; the safety of Flint did not. Builders of the new pipeline couldn't wait another season to start construction. Higher-ups in Flint said plant operators would be "heroes" by starting on time. Short of manpower, the plant had moved a handful of personnel from its waste collection department to the plant without training. Cost cutters chose to pay overtime rather than hire more staff.

When the plant started up, one county drain official, David Jansen, described the scene as "water out of control."

The plant staff tried. They raised and lowered chemical dosages, though researchers later wondered at their thinking. In its raw state, the Flint River contained just about everything imaginable, including untreated refuse from car factories, raw sewage, agricultural runoff, and toxics from leaching landfills. Operators could choose from some forty different chemicals for treatment.

The infinite number of chemical interactions exceeded the know-how of staff. And they lacked state-of-the-art equipment to monitor the effects of their additives. A logbook later showed that instead of using a pump to add polymers to water, employees took to "putting it on the second floor in the mechanical room and feeding through a hole in the floor."

As complaints piled up, operators inadvertently made everything worse. They faced the problem of bacteria breeding from the

The Flint water tower became a much-photographed symbol of the crisis.

organic matter in the river—the floaty particles from dead leaves or weeds, human or animal waste. The river contained more organic matter than the Great Lakes.

Operators had increased chlorine to kill off the bacteria, with the unintended consequence of producing cancer-causing byproducts, or TTHMs. In March of 2015, following the faulty advice of a water consultant hired by the city, plant operators turned to a coagulant, or thickener—ferric chloride—to help trap and eliminate organic matter. The consultant instructed Flint to double the dose.

But government guidelines warn that ferric chloride can increase

corrosion of old pipes. By adding the compound, Flint operators accelerated corrosion. By the end of the summer of 2015, a
researcher found, Flint's treated water was up to 100 percent more
corrosive than the raw river water meandering along nearby.

Top: Brenda Briggs, of Flint, pushes a grocery cart of bottled water received from a distribution site several blocks from her home. Many elders have struggled to manage the cost and physical challenge of obtaining bottled water. *Bottom*: Darline Long, of Flint, embraces her daughter, Wendy, at a Super 8 Motel in Burton, Michigan. The family makes the trip, when they can afford it, in order to bathe outside of city limits and to bond over the trauma of the water crisis.

9

Trust Fall

In March of 2015 the City of Flint tried harder to address the public outcry. The city formed citizen and expert advisory committees and hired professionals to contain the tense public meetings. Before he left his position, the emergency manager, Darnell Earley, hired the water consulting company Veolia for $40,000 to evaluate the plant setup, solve the TTHM violations, and offer advice on water treatment. The state would later sue Veolia and one other company, Lockwood, Andrews & Newman, Inc., for their apparently inadequate assessments. Parts of the suit were dismissed. In its defense, Veolia said it wasn't paid to analyze lead, only chlorine and bacteria. Emails later showed Veolia officials worried aloud about lead in Flint's water but never told Flint.

Trust waned bit by bit, measurable in small cracks and break-ages, in citizen complaints and public protests, pallets of plastic bot-tles, and calls for action from the pulpit on Sunday morning. No professional meeting or consulting firm could win it back.

In its absence, Flint adapted to a no-trust way of life.

Flint had already started boiling water. Boiled water was safe water, all assumed. LeeAnne Walters's daughter, Kaylie, faithfully boiled batches of tap water throughout 2014. She boiled it, let it cool, transferred it into gallon jugs, and put them in the refrigerator. She and her three younger siblings gulped down the water all summer long. Walters encouraged all her children to hydrate. Water was better than juice or soda. Wasn't that what health officials always stressed? And Kaylie liked to reach for water in place of snacks as a way to control her weight.

By January, Kaylie and her mother and the rest of Flint learned that boiling water likely intensified its harm. Cancer-causing chemical byproducts had circulated in the water since May. Boiling would only increase concentrations of the byproducts and of heavy metals. Why hadn't anyone told them? All across town, Flint institutions were also growing wary. In early 2015 the state treasury announced the installation of water coolers on every floor of the state office building in Flint, prompting state water officials to acknowledge a problem: how could one arm of the state offer "alternative" water to employees while another arm swore Flint tap water was safe? The coolers arrived anyway, illustrations of hypocrisy. The move hardly inspired faith in Flint water.

In January of 2015, the University of Michigan–Flint campus did its own water testing, discovered two water fountains with high levels of lead, and shut those down. In February, the Head Start programs for 1,300 preschoolers in Flint turned off their taps in favor of bottled water. The same month the Flint Children's Museum blocked its drinking fountains.

Residents, too, shut off their taps. They began lugging home plastic-wrapped cases of bottled water for every household need: from boiling an egg to watering plants and pouring water for puppies. How do you shower in bottled water? Marquez Williams devised a method. He punched pinholes in the bottle, then held it over his head and squeezed. E. Yvonne Lewis, founder and CEO of the National Center for African American Health Consciousness and a community health advocate, set up her Crock-Pot in the bathroom. That way she could heat bottled water without hauling a boiling pot from the stove.

Cases of water disappeared from grocery shelves faster than stores could restock them. Families began bathing and showering at fitness clubs or friends' and relatives' homes outside of Flint. Some resorted to bottled-water sponge baths, baby wipes, or "speed showers." And they watched tap water eat away water heaters, dishwashers, and washing machines. Who could afford to replace those? Carma Lewis's family on the north side replaced their washing machine twice; they relied on cold water for more than two years before they replaced their water heater.

Mistrust placed greater demands on the frail or fragile. Residents hauled cases and jugs of water from store to home to kitchen stove to bathroom sink to tub. If you were infirm or housebound, you relied on the kindness of strangers for water delivery or, more often, drank from the toxic tap. It was difficult for Carolyn Shannon, the elder who spoke often at council meetings. She could go to the store and buy the water and have an employee load it into her car. But when she got home, she was unable to haul the cases indoors. Her daughter finally bought her a large bottled-water dispenser, but she struggled with cooking. Shannon had tried rinsing off all the parts of her Thanksgiving turkey with bottled water, but found it nearly impossible.

The hardships of using bottled spelled a boon to private

water-delivery services, companies that truck cases or five-gallon jugs of purified, distilled, or spring water to a customer's door. In Flint, Culligan signed up scores of new customers and sold whole-house filters for those who could afford the $5,000 or so to install them. Shucon Hall, a Flint resident and single working mother and student, signed up for Culligan Water delivery only to learn the five-gallon jugs, in her neighborhood, had the value of liquid gold. They disappeared from her front steps while she was away at work or school. She began picking up the forty-pound jugs from Culligan directly, then carting them into her house, sometimes with the help of her young son. "You are the man, the water man," Hall told him.

Between work and school and without nearby family, Hall couldn't always keep up with her family's water demands. That's when she'd get a call from her three thirsty children, home after school to find the water cooler dry.

They knew the rules. You did not drink out of the faucet, ever. It was liquid poison. They had seen on YouTube how the water made you sick, gave you rashes, fed your rage, slowed your brain, stopped your growth. They had classmates like that. So on the days when the cooler was empty, the three set out together for the local convenience store where they shopped for the best beverage deal. Water came in mere sixteen-ounce containers, while soda and juice were sold in two-liter bottles for less. They chose juice or soda—while their momma paid for bottled and tap. They were among a generation of Flint children who recoiled from tap water.

Juice and soda were not healthy, Hall's children knew. Her daughter, Deszire, well understood the roughly $300 monthly cost of water for the household. They paid for river water and now they also paid Culligan.

Three students, silhouetted, sing holiday songs in front of water fountains warning, "Do Not Drink Until Further Notice," at Doyle-Ryder Elementary in Flint.

As her children made do at home, Hall took a job fielding complaints at the information desk across from the water department at Flint City Hall. She listened as desperate or enraged residents charged through city hall doors waving $5,000 and $7,000 water bills along with shutoff notices and house liens. They vented to Hall and sometimes made threats. Anyone who worked at city hall was suspect. A police officer periodically sat at the information desk. Hall understood all too well, she told residents. She could barely pay her own water bills.

In March of 2015, Veolia issued an eleven-page report. They recommended steps to improve Flint water that involved adding and subtracting chemicals, training staff, and improving communications with the public. But the report gave no hint of alarm. It said Flint water was "in compliance with State and Federal regulations, and based on those standards, the water is considered to meet drinking water requirements."

Few people in Flint felt reassured, and while officials tried to promote Flint water as clean, the community understood that it was toxic. They began to help one another. Grocery stores offered discounts on bottled water while churches, small businesses, and nonprofits gave away bottles for free. One giveaway, by a nonprofit dedicated to the reintegration of former convicts, ran through their supply in twenty minutes.

The community aid tracked with a mounting citizen backlash. More Facebook groups popped up and political coalitions came together. People marched in the streets. An especially defining protest took place during a bitterly cold, windy Valentine's Day march up Saginaw Street, where about fifty people shivered together. Flint resident Jessica Owens told a *Flint Journal* reporter that she didn't believe the water had improved. Hers had a "sewer" smell and was discolored. Residents ought to stop paying their bills. "It's water," she said. "It's not like we're talking about something for leisure. We need it for human life."

≋

Despite the disaster of the first town hall meeting at the Dome in January, the city tried again, but through a different tack. It selected members of the community to advise city officials, presumably to counteract the free-for-all feel at the Dome. In March the city held its first advisory committee meeting to talk about water, and this time it hired facilitators trained to preside. The professionals made little headway.

At that first session, held in a conference room at the local municipal bus station, shouting broke out. A woman prayed, a man silently held up photos of his brown water in protest, and a third resident was escorted out by police when he yelled that the water was killing him. The next committee meeting, at the public library, led to people jumping to their feet and chanting, "Answer the question!"

It was too late. A woman, Jaqueline Hill, called out, "You all are lying to us." The thin thread of goodwill that had held the community together had snapped. Mistrust replaced it—and spread like an epidemic of its own.

Suspicion fed upon itself. One young woman, Whitney Frierson, an activist and singer, had heard about Flint-area recalls of tainted bottled water. Friend Ty Belin reported that rumor back to his family on the north side of Flint. That prompted Ty and his family to take every precaution. They filtered their bottled water by pouring it through a Brita filter. Or they filtered tap water twice. It wasn't crazy. E. Yvonne Lewis, the community health advocate, had heard that a single filter did not ensure safe water. The only safe practice was to filter at least twice.

By the end of March 2015 the city council voted seven to one to reconnect to Detroit water, echoing what looked to be the overwhelming sentiment of Flint voters. But Gerald Ambrose's was the only vote that counted, and he voted no. "Incomprehensible," he said. "Flint water today is safe." A return to Detroit would cost too much, he steadfastly maintained. So the state held firm, water devoured the pipes, bacteria broke free, and public faith in government ebbed and slipped out of sight.

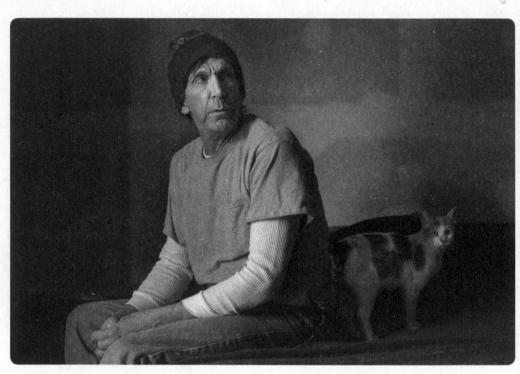

Tim Monahan of Flint contracted Legionnaires' disease in July 2014. He spiked a fever of 105.8 and was finally hospitalized and packed in ice.

10

"The Big Red Flag"

Smelly water and angry meetings were not the only sequels to the April 2014 switch to Flint River water. On a parallel track, a more deadly bacterium began to sicken and kill people in and around Flint. The outbreak was large, but it remained unknown to the public. Its almost secret unfolding would later reveal similar instances of government inaction, cover-up, and carelessness.

Tim Monahan, a fifty-seven-year-old carpenter, became one early victim. Monahan had dragged himself, exhausted and weak, to his job fixing a neighbor's roof in Flint in the early summer of 2014. Already lean, Monahan noticed that he was shedding weight. On July 3, his face gaunt and sunken, Monahan spiked a fever of more than 104°F. He went to the hospital only to have doctors there send him home. "Maybe heat stroke or heat prostration," Monahan said to his partner.

On July 4, the same day that Johnny Muhammad lugged water

from a gushing broken water main for his three children and Bishop Bernadel Jefferson watched her extended family develop rashes after swimming, Tim Monahan watched fireworks from the front porch of his Flint home. He sat in ninety-degree heat, wrapped in two heavy blankets and wearing a knit cap. He shivered violently and shared with his loved ones that he was "miserable, absolutely miserable."

By the next morning Monahan's fever shot up to 105.8°F. He returned to urgent care where doctors suspected a summer flu. This time Monahan refused to leave. Once admitted to the hospital he spent four days packed in ice. One morning a doctor arrived with four residents trailing him. While they spoke to him, the sickly Monahan coughed spontaneously into a nearby receptacle. An eager resident jumped forward. "I'll take that," the resident said.

The doctor had the sample cultured and returned the next day. "I don't know where you got this but you've got Legionnaires' disease," he told Monahan.

Monahan had heard of it, vaguely. The disease was named after a mysterious illness that sickened a group of people attending an American Legion convention at a Philadelphia hotel in 1976. That was all Monahan knew. At the hospital he was treated with antibiotics and remained there for nine days. Once released he learned more.

Legionnaires' disease is caused by bacteria that naturally reside in fresh water, often in pond scum in lakes and rivers. A polluted river will have many quiet eddies and backwaters where scum, and *Legionella*, the bacteria behind the disease, may flourish.

Corroded water systems are also playgrounds for *Legionella* growth. In systems with corrosion control, bacteria may live safely away from human ingestion inside of sticky substances clinging to pipe interiors known as biofilms. The buildup of interior scale (with corrosion control) ordinarily protects the biofilms. But when untreated water corrodes metal pipes, biofilms may also be stripped away, releasing bacteria into the water stream. And water main breaks that stop and start the flow of water through corroded pipes also increase the corrosion of the biofilms.

As if that were not enough chemical and bacterial mayhem, iron interacts with chloride by neutralizing it; therefore, adding chlorine to kill *Legionella* in a corroded system may not do the job. Meanwhile, iron is known to boost *Legionella* growth. As US water systems have aged, the incidence of *Legionella* has also increased.

Legionella may be

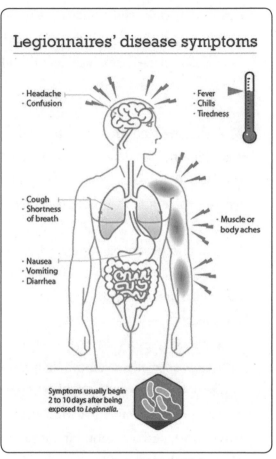

Legionnaires' disease produces severe pneumonia-like symptoms and can be difficult to diagnose. The disease derives from the *Legionella* bacteria, which grows naturally in the environment and flourishes in warm water.

inhaled in water droplets or vapor and in places like hot tubs, showers, air-conditioning systems, humidifiers, and supermarket produce sprayers.

And these bacteria can kill people. Legionnaires' is a serious form of pneumonia accompanied by fever, vomiting, nausea, diarrhea, and extreme weakness, among other symptoms. It is especially deadly in people who smoke or who already suffer from some other debilitating illnesses like diabetes, kidney disease, or cancer. And *Legionella* bacteria can also lead to milder respiratory disease.

≋

Monahan had no idea how he had contracted Legionnaires' disease. No one he knew in his home or circle of friends or family had ever had the disease. Yet in the halls of government, a very long list of people knew—in at least three states, four cities, and eight government offices. In all, dozens of health and water protectors knew that a deadly bacterium was harming Flint. It became one of the largest outbreaks of Legionnaires' in US history, and one that flourished and then ebbed in perfect sync with the water switch. But Flint didn't know.

Later, experts said the silence was bewildering and highly unusual, especially given the high number of cases. New York City suffered a similar outbreak over a parallel period in 2015, leading to public announcements within weeks—and regular updates. Flint, by contrast, revealed nothing, at least until about eighteen months after Monahan grew ill.

There had been suspicions even before Monahan's diagnosis in early July 2014. In late June, at a monthly Flint meeting of doctors and public health officials concerned with communicable diseases, a county worker shared information about what might be a Legionnaires' spike. The previous year there had been eight cases in total. Ordinarily the number ranged from two to nine annually. Already in June, the worker reported, there had been six reported cases.

As summer unfolded, the data continued to point to an outbreak. In July, there were five more cases. In August, another ten. By the end of 2014, there were forty-two cases of Legionnaires' disease confirmed in Genesee County—surpassing the number of cases from the previous four years combined. By comparison, no surrounding counties saw any spikes.

The numbers correlated closely with Flint's switch to river water. But emails showed at least one state water supervisor cared first about not blaming the river on the outbreak. "She was concerned that we were going to be making some announcement soon about the water being the source of infection," wrote a state health department worker to county health workers. "I told her the Flint water was at this point just a hypothesis."

But common sense had already prompted county health workers to look to the river. Jim Henry, a mild-mannered county environmental health supervisor new to the job, had a strong hunch that the outbreak had somehow derived from the river switch. "That was the big red flag," Henry later said in court. "Stickin' out like a sore thumb. We needed to check the water in that system."

He knew he needed to map the outbreak to find out. Who was getting sick where? To do so he would need data from the City of Flint. Henry asked for the data in late fall of 2014. He called and wrote to the City of Flint without any response. Frustrated, he filed a Freedom of Information request—a legal document that requires public agencies to release public information by law. With it, he pressed the need: "This is rather glaring information and it needs to be looked into now," Henry urged, "prior to the warmer summer months when Legionella is at its peak and we are potentially faced with a crisis."

Henry, a dark-haired, heavyset man, worried especially about a second outbreak since *Legionella* thrives in warm water. The county's cases had always clustered around the summertime and early fall. He called his request a "significant and urgent public health issue." He said Flint's earlier known drinking water violations, the TTHMs, "pale in comparison to the potential public health risks of Legionella."

When, in March of 2015, Henry had still heard nothing from Flint, his boss went to city hall. He told Flint's emergency manager, Gerald Ambrose, and the mayor, Dayne Walling, about the outbreak of Legionnaires' disease. By then, five people had died of the disease. He told the Flint officials that fact, too.

Tim Monahan, released from the hospital, was as weak and tired as an old dog. He had lost twenty pounds. His construction job had to wait another three or four weeks for him to regain his strength, and even then he worked only for an hour or two at a time. His nine-year-old niece, Chadie, who lived with Monahan and his partner since her mother's death, had witnessed her uncle's decline with great concern. She had had to wear a mask to visit him at the hospital, and it was all she could do to keep from crying. She was terribly worried that she would lose another person she loved. Once her uncle came home, she knew he was too weak for piggyback rides. She worried when he began coughing and couldn't stop.

During his hospital stay Monahan had received a call from an epidemiologist from the federal Centers for Disease Control. "Just

trying to figure out, where'd you get this?" the scientist asked, following up with questions about what buildings or restaurants or
businesses he had visited. Monahan didn't really know. As far as
Monahan knew, he was the only person around who had been diagnosed with Legionnaires'.

≋

As people struggled for breath in intensive care units, bureaucrats
pinged emails around the chain. A few stood out for their urgency.
In February of 2015 a county epidemiologist in Flint, Shurooq
Hasan, wrote to the CDC seeking help. The number of cases had
risen to forty-seven, "almost four times the number of cases we had
during 2013, and the highest number of cases [of any] county in the
state for 2014." Hasan said the county had investigated a hospital as
a source but expanded their investigation "to include the city water
supply."

Hasan went on to describe how the people afflicted were so sick
that they were "unable to answer our questions when we investigate
due to the severity of their conditions once hospitalized."

The email blizzard continued. Henry, of the county health
department, reiterated his belief to state water regulators at the
Michigan Department of Environmental Quality that Flint water
was the source. The state DEQ, in turn, attacked the county: "This
is beyond irresponsible," said the DEQ's public relations chief, Brad
Wurfel. He accused Henry of not doing his job. Another official,
Stephen Busch, who had written the memo two years earlier about
why the Flint River was a bad idea, now wrote up reasons for why
Legionnaires' wasn't his office's problem. "Nicely done," his boss
told him.

By now the EPA's Del Toral, the expert who had consulted with mother-scientist LeeAnne Walters about lead, told the state that Flint water could easily be the source of the *Legionella* bacteria, especially given Flint's constant flushing of pipes, which would only help strip their interior coating and loosen more bacteria. The state found Del Toral annoying and sought to silence him. "If he continues to persist," the DEQ's Busch wrote to colleagues, "we may need [higher authorities] to make a call to EPA to help address his over-reaches."

Busch's colleague chimed in: "I agree, the constant second guessing of how we interpret and implement our rules is getting tiresome."

Meanwhile, outside the state, the federal CDC in Atlanta wrote to Michigan officials with alarm. "We are very concerned," an epidemiologist wrote to the county and state regarding the outbreak. "It's very large, one of the largest we know of in the past decade, and community-wide, and in our opinion and experience it needs a comprehensive investigation."

Henry hoped that meant a federal team of experts would finally descend on the county to help. But instead the state health department stepped in and reprimanded the county for violating chain-of-command rules. Asking for help from the CDC "really should be at the request of the state," the higher-up said, "rather than the local health department." And besides, there was no need, the official continued. He had "not seen any information that would rise to the level of warranting" such a request.

Jim Henry felt stymied. The days were warming, and that meant the water was as well. He was racing against the seasonal clock. At the end of May, Henry received a state report declaring the Legionnaires' disaster over. He thought it was a misprint. But no—the report, from the Michigan Department of Health and Human Services, said it plainly: "The outbreak is over; the last reported case occurred in March, 2015."

That observation turned out to be grievously premature. In June 2015, seven new cases of Legionnaires' disease surfaced. One person died. In July, thirteen more cases were reported—and three more people died. In August, another thirteen cases came to light; that month another three people died of Legionnaires'. And in September, another nine cases were reported. In total about ninety people were sickened and at least twelve people died from Legionnaires' over the course of the switch to Flint River water.

Later, news outlets, researchers, and activist groups filed flurries of requests to see the trail of government correspondence to determine who knew what and when. Some revealed Flint emergency managers knew as early as October of 2014. Lawsuits later named a hospital, McLaren Flint, an apparent point of contact for many Legionnaires' patients. Researchers hired by the state identified the Flint River as the likely source. At least one outside expert concurred, explaining how chlorine, neutralized by organic matter, had no doubt failed to kill off bacteria. The hospital? It was "a big building sitting on a broken system," the expert said.

Jim Henry stuck with his plainspoken assessment. Deaths could have been avoided, he said. The state's passivity had been "criminal." But he said that he, too, had erred: in placing his own trust in Michigan officials. He said he knew why the state had been passive and hostile. They "were concerned that Genesee County's largest U.S. Legionella outbreak would implicate the Flint water system, for which they were responsible."

The state, he said, reminded him of "a stubborn [two-year-old] child." That child had been caught in a lie and decided to make up bigger lies instead of admitting the truth.

"Instead of doing what is right," he added, "they'll willfully take another spanking just to be defiant."

〜〜

Tim Monahan learned only one-and-a-half years after he became ill that his Legionnaires' was likely tied to the Flint River. The Michigan governor's office didn't publicly announce the outbreak until January 2016. Monahan was stunned. "Not once did anyone hint that there was a spike, that there were more cases," he told reporters who came to ask. "None of us knew, none of us knew what was going on."

To this day, Monahan says the Legionnaires' victims are the forgotten ones. He has never met a fellow survivor and there is no registry or clearinghouse. It sometimes feels as if it never happened. "No one talks about us anymore," he said. Yet Monahan has never recovered. He used to work long days building houses, something he's been unable to do since his bout with the disease.

That so many people fell ill and died while so many others knew was horrific, disastrous, a "ridiculous tragedy," Monahan said. His niece, Chadie, thought of the families in Flint whose loved ones didn't make it, and who didn't even know what had happened until the government announced their findings some eighteen months after the outbreak. With her brow creased with concern, Chadie tried to put herself in their shoes: "I just can't imagine how those other families felt."

REPLY TO THE ATTENTION OF:

WG-15J

June 24, 2015

MEMORANDUM

SUBJECT: High Lead Levels in Flint, Michigan – Interim Report

FROM: Miguel A. Del Toral
Regulations Manager, Ground Water and Drinking Water Branch

TO: Thomas Poy
Chief, Ground Water and Drinking Water Branch

The purpose of this interim report is to summarize the available information regarding activities conducted to date in response to high lead levels in drinking water reported by a resident in the City of Flint, Michigan. The final report will be submitted once additional analyses have been completed on pipe and water samples.

Following a change in the water source, the City of Flint has experienced a number of water quality issues resulting in violations of National Primary Drinking Water Regulations (NPDWR) including acute and non-acute Coliform Maximum Contaminant Level (MCL) violations and Total Trihalomethanes (TTHM) MCL violations as follows:

Acute Coliform MCL violation in August 2014
Monthly Coliform MCL violation in August 2014
Monthly Coliform MCL violation in September 2014
Average TTHM MCL violation in December 2014
Average TTHM MCL violation in June 2015

In addition, as of April 30, 2014, when the City of Flint switched from purchasing finished water from the City of Detroit to using the Flint River as their new water source, the City of Flint is no longer providing corrosion control treatment for lead and copper.

A major concern from a public health standpoint is the absence of corrosion control treatment in the City of Flint for mitigating lead and copper levels in the drinking water. Recent drinking water sample results indicate the presence of high lead results

In June 2015, a government expert on public water systems, Miguel Del Toral, circulated a multipage memo foretelling grave dangers to Flint residents without proper treatment of river water.

11

A Whistle Blows

Miguel Del Toral's graying beard and receding hairline were turning grayer and more recessive with the utter lack of urgency everywhere he turned. After the phone call in April 2015, LeeAnne Walters had immediately sent him the list of Flint water additives—the list she had already read to him, verbatim, three times over the phone. He called her back. "Oh my god," he said to Walters, "they are not using any corrosion control."

Drinking water experts in Michigan had told Del Toral in writing that they were using an "optimized corrosion control program," whatever that was. The documents in front of Del Toral told him that their idea of "optimized" was to have done nothing. Maybe the list had missed something. Del Toral wrote to the state staff again, asking what, exactly, Flint was using for corrosion control.

That's when the official answer changed. By late April of 2015 it was clear to Del Toral that the state was using nothing to control pipe corrosion. Nor did the water protectors at the state DEQ seem concerned. They were conducting their own lead and copper tests every six months, and those looked fine. Anyway, Flint would be returning to Lake Huron water as soon as that pipeline was completed. Flint could simply run out the clock until the hookup down the road.

Meanwhile, at the Walters home lead levels continued to spiral upward. Walters's first lead test had prompted a "WOW" from a federal worker at the 104 ppb measure. In March Walters's water tested at a triple "WOW"—397 ppb of lead, followed by a mind-boggling 707 ppb. That's when the water was shut off and the garden hoses were put in place for bathing and laundering only. Now Walters's family of six was drinking bottled, and the cases on their enclosed front porch grew to the windowsill and lined the walls.

From Del Toral's point of view, it should have been obvious by now that an entire city was being poisoned. He pleaded with superiors to do something. He contacted officials in Michigan state offices. He later ranted to colleagues, calling his own agency a "cesspool" of incompetence for failing to act.

Del Toral believed Flint officials were masking true lead counts by the hydrant and tap flushing before collecting samples. Fudging the numbers and then not warning the public bordered on "criminal neglect," he warned.

Basic science predicted what was surely happening: no corrosion control combined with old lead lines equaled lead poisoning and *Legionella* growth. Common sense would dictate that the Walters home was one of many, not the only one. The state had argued that an unusual hookup to an old lead line made the Walters home an anomaly. Del Toral disagreed. "We don't need to drop a bowling ball off every building in every town to know that it will fall to the ground in all of these places," Del Toral wrote. He even offered to fund his own trip to Flint to take samples to establish a pattern. Del Toral was rebuffed.

Protesters gather in May 2015 outside a local TV news station, demanding the city switch back to Detroit water. The march continued down Saginaw Street and ended at the Flint Farmers' Market.

At the end of June, Del Toral blasted the loudest alarm he could muster. He wrote a detailed, eight-page memo with the subject line "High Lead Levels in Flint, Michigan" to the EPA's head of drinking water for all the Great Lakes. He copied drinking water officials in Michigan and EPA water experts in Cincinnati, as well as a friend and expert on lead in drinking water at Virginia Tech.

He detailed five water violations in Flint—the three bacterial violations that had led to the boil water advisories as well as two TTHM violations. He said the lack of corrosion control was "a major concern from a public health standpoint." High lead readings from resident samples were also a "serious concern." Plant operators had added one chemical, ferric chloride, that was known to increase lead corrosion. And two professional consulting firms who had conducted surveys of Flint water in 2014 and 2015 had failed to address the potential interactions between corrosion and lead poisoning.

He described his findings. He said testing at LeeAnne Walters's home had revealed lead so high, at 13,200 ppb, that it exceeded measures of toxic waste. He said one of Walters's children had tested positive for lead. And he warned that Flint was likely using faulty data, since their five-minute preflushing practice lowered lead measurements. The state had also dropped from its samples homes with the highest readings, like Walters's. It looked like the state was cheating.

Now, on paper at least, eight federal and state water officials knew of Del Toral's alarm.

As a courtesy, Del Toral also slipped a copy to Walters.

Subject: Flint Water Complaint
From: "Busch, Stephen (DEQ)" <BUSCHS@michigan.gov>
Date: 10/14/2014 1:54 PM
To: "rbincsik@cityofflint.com" <rbincsik@cityofflint.com>
CC: "Brent Wright (bwright@cityofflint.com)" <bwright@cityofflint.com>, "Prysby, Mike (DEQ)" <PRYSBYM@michigan.gov>

Rob,

We have been forwarded the following complaint information from EPA. Could you please let us know whether you have received their complaint and provide a summary of any action or communication with the complaintant? Thanks.

Citizen lives at 324 West Jackson Avenue, Flint, 48505

She states, "Water quality is bad since switching to Flint River. My water stinks like sewage at times. I have developed a cough and rash, brown sediment in sink basins and kitchen sink stays backed up. I have written City Hall Water Dept and Council President for help, but no response. "

Stephen Busch, P.E.
Lansing and Jackson District Supervisor
Office of Drinking Water and Municipal Assistance
MDEQ
517-643-2314

Many Flint complaints fell into a bureaucratic abyss. One resident wrote to the city's water department and council president before taking her unanswered concerns to the federal Environmental Protection Agency. The EPA in turn forwarded the letter to the State of Michigan, where Stephen Busch, a drinking water supervisor, sent this 2014 complaint back to the city, full circle.

12

Denial

Miguel Del Toral had presented credible science and an expert's urgent concern to state and federal water regulators. On the ground in Flint, residents had come together in sustained protests at city hall and the state capitol. A reasonable person might have expected immediate action. Instead, an EPA ethics officer told Del Toral he was not to speak with anyone from Flint or about Flint again.

"What did I do wrong?" Del Toral wanted to know.

With Del Toral silenced, Flint complaints were handed off to the EPA's Jennifer Crooks, who handled them with disdain. "Yep, another complaint about our favorite water supply :). Let me tell you, this Flint situation is a nasty issue—I've had people call me using four letter words, calling me a crook, but I'm developing a thicker skin."

When a radio reporter who got wind of the document inquired with the State of Michigan, a DEQ spokesman told Flint to calm down.

"Let me start here," the spokesman, Brad Wurfel, said confidently. "Anyone who is concerned about lead in the drinking water in Flint can relax." He added that the report had been written by a "rogue employee" and Del Toral's final, vetted version would tell a very different story.

Del Toral's boss at the EPA also downplayed the whistleblower's investigative report. When Flint's mayor asked for a copy and wondered in writing whether there was any cause for worry, the EPA boss told him the report wasn't ready and apologized. She wished him a happy Fourth of July.

A few days later, Mayor Walling went on television, where a local news anchor handed him a mug of Flint water. Walling tipped it back, drank it down, and said it was safe. "It's your standard tap water," he told viewers. "You can taste a little bit of the chlorine."

Inside state government, Wurfel was telling the governor's office the water was technically within regulations. "The bottom line is that residents of Flint do not need to worry about lead in their water supply," Wurfel wrote to the governor's staff in a memo. He said that, by law, Flint had eighteen months to evaluate whether it needed to fix corrosion, and then another two years to implement the plan. By then the new pipeline would be in place. There was just no point.

Like global warming or the harm of tobacco, Flint's poisoning was hard to face and easier to deny. State and national reporters didn't advance the story, essentially taking Wurfel and the rest of the state at its word. A veteran statehouse reporter later acknowledged as much: "I think it's fair to say that collectively, this was not the media's greatest shining moment."

Only the local *Flint Journal* and Michigan Radio could claim early and active coverage. Others had fallen into a trap—interviewing activists, seeking an official denial, and then leaving the news at that.

Nayyirah Shariff had tried to alert the reporters about what she knew. She later surmised that the media was too quick to accept the state's word. If the state said Flint water was safe, that surely trumped any citizen complaint. Journalists, Shariff said, had been "bamboozled by their own perceived intelligence."

The same denial blinded doctors. Dr. Mona Hanna-Attisha, a Flint pediatrician, spent more than a year reassuring her pediatric patients and their mothers. "Don't waste your money on bottled water," she told one mother and child. "They say it is fine to drink."

And many Flint citizens wished away the possibility of poisoning, especially if their water's taste set off no alarms. Some grew tired of the work or lacked the resources required to avoid the tap. How did a large family cope? E. Yvonne Lewis was feeling neighborly one day after the switch, when she found herself with more bottled water than she could use. She walked some over to the family of six living next door.

"I'm sorry," said her neighbor. "I can't take any more because I can't do this anymore. It's too overwhelming. I'm just going to use tap water." Her children followed her choice. If their mother didn't think it was a problem, they needn't bother. Two of her daughters were later diagnosed with lead poisoning, Lewis said. Which didn't mean only two had been harmed.

"The entire family is traumatized," said Lewis.

Protesters gather outside of the Flint Farmers' Market in May 2015.

13

Convergence

In late spring and summer of 2015 in Flint, little had changed. The olive-colored river warmed, bacteria bloomed, heavy metals broke free of rusted pipes and whisked into Flint homes. Above ground, testimonials of suffering piled higher, including at the Michigan Office of the Attorney General, which so far in 2015 had received more than a dozen emotional pleas from Flint—from a mother of two young children, from a paraplegic and elderly grandmother, from elected officials. "My hair is falling out, my skin is disgusting, and my dog was sick until we switched her to bottled water," one complainant wrote. "We need help in Flint PLEASE."

The cries for help, though, went unanswered. The apathy shown by the government guardians of water served to kindle further outrage. Flint residents pulled together and pushed back around a common goal: return to Great Lakes water.

Flint clergy had grasped the problem from the earliest days

following the switch to the river. Reverend Alfred Harris, the bespectacled and crisply dressed president of Concerned Pastors for Social Action, had functioned as an unofficial office of citizen complaint on Sunday mornings at his Saints of God Church, never doubting congregants' stories of losing hair, breaking out in skin rashes, and turning on black tap water that smelled like sewage or mothballs. Many pastors had heard the stories. Harris had stopped baptisms for fear of the tap water.

"We have witnessed their anxiety and felt their anger," Harris wrote in the *Courier*, a newspaper covering Flint-area churches. Harris and other members of Concerned Pastors had traveled to Lansing to speak with the governor's office.

In April of 2015, Harris stood behind a podium in the light-filled atrium of Flint City Hall in front of the Department of Finance, where residents paid their water bills. His was a moral plea to return

Residents shout in agreement as David Bullock, a Detroit pastor, addresses the water crisis during a rally at Bethel United Methodist Church in January 2016.

to Great Lakes water. "We are not framing our argument in *money*!" said Harris, who rocked on his feet and waved his hands emphatically and then snapped his fingers, gesturing as if for cash. "We are framing our argument in the *health issue*!"

"*Yes!*" the crowd of pastors, parents, activists, and a city councilman called out and applauded.

"Why don't we do what's *ethically* right?"

"Amen!"

"And I believe what's *morally* right!"

"*Yes!*"

"What's *spiritually* right!"

"Yes!"

"And get back to the purest source that God has blessed us with."

"Yes."

"And come *together*!"

"*That's right.*"

"And make it *work*."

But down the hall in the emergency manager's office, Gerald Ambrose, the white and white-haired emergency manager, refused. Detroit water was no safer than Flint water, he asserted. And reconnecting to Detroit water cost too much. It was, he added for emphasis, "not going to happen." A few weeks later, Ambrose left the job. It had been difficult, he told a Michigan Radio reporter on his way out. You couldn't eliminate city services without affecting "real people," he said. There were limitations to radical cost-cutting. "A city cannot help its people if it is itself broke," he said.

"There's just a point in time there's just not enough gas in the tank," Ambrose added. "There's just not enough revenue from the local taxpayers to solve the problems that are here. Whether the city's here or not, the people will be here. And they're going to have some basic needs that have to be met, one way or another."

≈

At an early June 2015 city council meeting, Gertrude Marshall approached the microphone in the council chamber. She was dressed in a white T-shirt and wore her hair in a black-and-white-print bandana. She began quietly, conversationally. "I'm here today because I've broken out with that rash again," she said. "That I got from the water. It was gone, completely. Now it has returned. You guys are telling us that the water is OK. The water is not OK. It's still not OK. Please, fix the water."

Marshall twisted to her right, facing a man in the front row, Howard Croft, the head of Flint's public utilities department. Croft wore a dark suit and red tie and held documents across his knees. Marshall seemed to be speaking to an old friend who had somehow lost his way, and she addressed him by name, her voice wobbly.

"Please clear up this water, Howard. This has affected me," Marshall said, explaining how, in nearly fifty years, she had never been to a hospital except to give birth to her six children. That had recently changed for the grandmother and childcare worker. "For my breath to be short like it is, there's something wrong," she told Croft, still looking at him directly, her tone rising. "For me to be as shaky as I am, there's something wrong. For this rash to return, there is something wrong, There's something wrong, Howard! Fix our water. Fix our water. *Stop* coming to us and telling us the water is *safe* when we're telling you something is *wrong with the water*."

Maybe Croft knew something that she did not, she allowed, but she could not ignore the assault on her body. She leaned forward, her voice rising as she urged a moral choice upon someone who didn't seem to hear. *"Fix it!"* she ordered Croft. "We need *water! We need* it! It's not something we *want! We need this! Our bodies need this! Do you understand that, Howard? Get this right!"*

Croft said nothing and the council president asked for the next speaker, but Marshall's one strong voice turned out to be part of an ever-widening chorus of voices and calls to action that merged together throughout the summer months of 2015. Pastors and activists filed an injunction to force Flint's return to Detroit water. They launched a petition drive with the same goal and delivered to Mayor Walling a stack of nearly 27,000 signatures from around the US and Canada calling for a reconnect to the Great Lakes.

Some state and national media—the *Detroit Free Press,* the *New York Times*—had written about the tense Dome meeting in January or the council vote in March. Six months later, though, neither had followed up. But a lone journalist had begun to gather enough information about Flint water to produce some deeper and more hard-hitting stories. The reporter, Curt Guyette, a lanky, earnest, and passionate investigator, had been hired by the American Civil Liberties Union in Michigan to chronicle the effects of the emergency management law. By late June, Guyette had collected enough video interviews to produce a minidocumentary about Flint water: *Hard to Swallow: Toxic Water Under a Toxic System in Flint.* The nearly six-minute video was released by the ACLU online, just as Guyette received a copy of Del Toral's red-alarm memo from Lee-Anne Walters. Guyette soon posted a story on the ACLU website about that, too.

A week later he wrote a similar piece for the *Nation.* In July, the *Atlantic* magazine published a feature story online that quoted mother and activist Melissa Mays: "I've never seen a first-world city have such disregard for human safety," she said.

In Flint, resistance spread. On the first anniversary of the water switch, about seventy people demonstrated at city hall. In June an umbrella organization, the Flint Coalition for Clean Water, filed a lawsuit claiming a "reckless disregard" for Flint families. In August, Flint's Concerned Pastors, this time with activists, returned to Lansing to meet with state drinking water staff.

During one emotional exchange, Melissa Mays and LeeAnne Walters tried handing a copy of the Del Toral memo to the manager of Michigan's office of drinking water. The DEQ manager, Liane Shekter-Smith, raised both hands in the air as if refusing a hot poker.

"I'm not touching [it]," said Shekter-Smith, according to court testimony. The witness, Laura Sullivan, a professor of mechanical engineering at Kettering University, said the Flint group was treated as if there were "no truth, no validity to anything they were saying."

Walters, in tears, begged the state official anyway. "Please take this," Walters said.

But the official refused.

At Walters's house, meanwhile, another national water expert had arrived on the scene. He was Professor Marc Edwards, a crusading scientist who specialized in public drinking water systems and corrosion. Edwards was a professor of civil engineering at Virginia Tech, and he had earned names in the press like "Water Guy" and "Corrosion Man" and "Professor of Plumbing." The lean, youthful-looking Edwards and the EPA's Del Toral had fought for years to expose government wrongdoing in a case of poisonous lead in water in Washington, DC. They had also talked about how to press the EPA to act in Flint.

When Edwards learned Del Toral and his memo had been side-lined, he grew "really, really angry," he later told a college crowd. Edwards knew lead levels measured at their highest in the middle of the night. He traveled to Flint and slept on Walters's couch to take samples. The highest result, 13,200 ppb, was the worst lead-in-water contamination Edwards had seen in his career. It was time to declare a war—on unethical science and engineering, as he saw it. A science war. "You don't fight a war to wound, you fight a war to win," he said.

Edwards began filing Freedom of Information requests, under the law that allows the public to access information produced by public bodies—to understand what had been going on behind the scenes. Soon he and the reporter Guyette, who filed his own requests, were able to document how state workers appeared to have tampered with the water-sampling results.

Guyette had grown frustrated by the roundabout nature of the water story. He made a conscious decision to abandon journalistic distance. He could no longer abide the mere gathering of quotations from opposing sources. He needed to break through the talking heads to find facts that would reveal the scope of contamination. One night at home he thought, "Oh well, Jeez, maybe we could do our own tests." His job included funds for research; maybe it could pay for mass testing. He called Edwards.

"How much does it cost for each test?" the reporter asked.

"Oh, seventy bucks," Edwards said.

"How many do you need—how many homes do you need to get a scientifically valid sample?"

Members of a civil rights group, New Era Detroit, assemble outside a Flint convenience store in February 2016 to hand out water while chanting "Power to the people."

"Fifty, at minimum," Edwards said. "Hundred would be better."

Guyette took the idea to Flint activists, and in August of 2015, a round-the-clock, citizen-scientist-journalist-pastor water relay commenced. It was a kaleidoscopic brigade. The Virginia Tech group sent three hundred water sampling kits to Harris's Saints of God church. There citizens picked up the testing kits and went door to door throughout the city to collect the samples. Soon the samples came back to the church.

"And then, as soon as the sample kits started being returned, twelve at a time, we'd box them up and send them back to Virginia Tech," Guyette later explained in an interview. "And they're working around the clock to get them analyzed, because as soon as they start seeing the results, they're going, 'Oh, no, this is bad. This is bad.' You know, by the time they got the first twenty-four bottles, they knew. There were so many with elevated levels that they knew that this was a crisis."

Edwards had expected to receive no more than a few dozen test kits back for testing. But in three weeks, Flint citizens had produced 277 samples, compared with the state's feeble seventy collected in a year. "It was unprecedented what the residents did," Guyette said. "No one had ever done a citizen-led test that was that extensive before."

Alarm bells sounded as results at the Virginia Tech labs revealed high lead levels in test after test of Flint water. At the lab, students and faculty began calling Flint residents with high lead in their water. "Stop drinking your water!" they told them. "It's dangerous!"

Edwards and his team also created a website to report the results in batches. The first batch showed "worrisome" results, the team wrote. The next batch of results were "concerning." Finally, once

252 samples had been tested, the Virginia Tech team virtually shouted out a warning in bold, red, and capitalized text: FLINT HAS A VERY SERIOUS LEAD IN WATER PROBLEM. Some 40 percent of samples tested above the federal limit for lead. The team kept calling Flint residents with their warning.

≈≈≈

September 15, 2015, felt like late summer in Flint, with cirrus clouds streaking across a faded blue sky. A diverse cluster of about twenty people stood before a media squad on the front lawn of sprawling Flint City Hall. Among the group were two scientists, an investigative reporter, some concerned parents, grassroots activists, a city councilman, and a group of pastors for social justice. The American and Michigan flags flapped lazily in the background. The group was multiracial, multicultural, multiaged. It was a landmark day for Flint, Melissa Mays began, a day to announce the "gut-punching" results of their collective work.

"Today is a huge, huge day for the water fight in Flint," said Mays, the parent-turned-activist and early cofounder, with Walters, of the Facebook group Water You Fighting For?

In twenty minutes, the press conference told a damning story of lead contamination, government incompetence, cheating, denial, and cover-up. LeeAnne Walters described the astronomical lead levels at her home and her lead-poisoned child.

Scientist Edwards produced a camera-ready experiment. He pulled from his left pocket a small glass bottle filled with Detroit water and held it high. Most cities, he said, put chemicals in their water to stop corrosion. "There's an iron nail in this bottle," he explained. Yet the water was clear.

From his right pocket, he fished out a bottle the same size. There was an iron nail in that bottle, too. Edwards spoke as he raised the second bottle into the air. "When we do the exact same thing with Flint water—"

He was interrupted as a collective "oh!" rippled through the crowd. The water in the Flint bottle was a burnt-orange color.

The Flint River water was much more highly corrosive than Detroit water, Edwards explained, with no corrosion control. "So this water looks bad, smells bad, it tastes bad," Edwards said.

Worse, as corrosive Flint water ate up old pipes from the inside out, it acted like sandpaper, scraping lead off the interior walls. You couldn't see lead the way you could iron, he explained. But on the basis of the testing conducted in Flint, his team had made an educated guess: "We estimate that the water in about 5,000 Flint homes is over the standard set by the World Health Organization for lead in water."

"Wow," the crowd murmured.

The corrosive water was accelerating the aging of Flint's water-distribution system by about twelve years, Edwards added, triggering many more water main breaks in the system, which likely hastened the sloughing off of the interior protective scale on the pipes. One day there were fourteen water main breaks.

The investigative reporter, Guyette, said the government was cheating the tests with preflushing. The testers cheated in other ways, too—by including sites with no or low contamination and throwing out the ones with more until the numbers read as acceptable. Guyette said it was time for a "full-fledged, independent, outside investigation."

Then Reverend Allen Overton stepped forward, representing the umbrella Coalition for Clean Water. Wearing a black suit, dark sunglasses, and a baseball cap, Overton called Flint's administration "criminal" and demanded a return to "the best water, the freshest water, the cleanest water" available, from the Great Lakes. "We cannot wait," he said. "They cannot continue to use us as their personal guinea pigs."

Nayyirah Shariff, among the most steadfast activists, stepped forward to name this seventeen-month-long experiment a public health crisis. She demanded free water filters for each tap in all homes to protect against lead. Dr. Laura Sullivan, the professor of engineering at Kettering, demanded the government locate every lead line, notify residents, and replace them at once.

And LeeAnne Walters wrapped up on a note of pure fury: "The bottom line is, *stop* trying to come up with ways to *hide* the lead!" she asserted to the cameras. "You should be *looking* for the high lead. That is your *job* at the DEQ. When you find it you *tell* us."

But that day the DEQ dismissed the data and claims. "The problem isn't new," spokesman Brad Wurfel told the *Flint Journal*. "It's just news [now, and] a knee-jerk reaction would be an irresponsible response."

Virginia Tech made the same claims everywhere, Wurfel said. The scientists "pull that rabbit out of that hat everywhere they go." They were just "fanning political flames irresponsibly." Meanwhile the City of Flint said it was following all government rules. They might as well have stuck their fingers in their ears and closed their eyes.

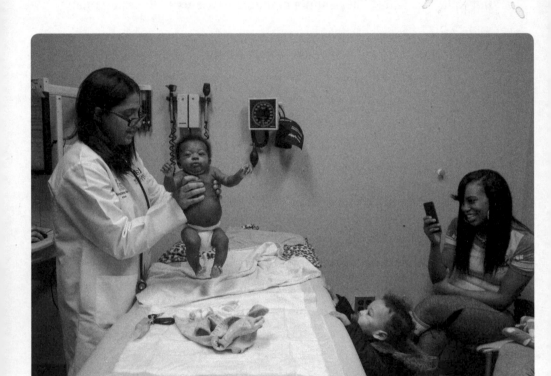

Dr. Mona Hanna-Attisha examines two-month-old Taeyana Brown while her mother, Quayana Towns, looks on. The pediatrician's research showed an alarming rise in Flint children's lead levels after the switch to the Flint River.

14

Blood Speaks

For about seventeen months, Dr. Mona Hanna-Attisha, the public-health oriented pediatrician at Hurley Medical Center in Flint, had told patients that Flint's stinky and sludge-like water was safe. "It's fine. Yes, it's fine. Drink the water," she had told pregnant women, nursing mothers, and parents of little kids. And when the pediatric residents she oversaw asked her what to tell Flint families, Dr. Mona, as she was called, reassured them, too. "Tap water is the best and safest," she said.

The compact and energetic young doctor wore black-framed glasses and her dark hair long and straight. She lived in a suburb of Detroit about an hour from Flint, where neither she nor her husband and two young children had the intimate day-to-day use of water that Flint residents did.

But Dr. Mona also had a history of environmental activism, which she attributed in part to her Iraqi American upbringing. In high school she helped to shut down a polluting incinerator near her home. In college she created an environmental health semester at the University of Michigan. As a pediatrician, she understood that kids' health was determined by where they lived. Life expectancy in one north end zip code in Flint was 64.7 years on average. In Ann Arbor, an hour to the south, residents in some neighborhoods lived twenty-four years longer, to eighty-nine. Within Flint itself, about eight miles could mean the difference between living to age sixty-four or seventy-nine, a difference of fifteen years. Many in Flint lived with the trauma of violence and the stress of racism or poverty, without access to adequate health care, fresh foods, transportation, or well-funded schools.

Dr. Mona had followed the April 2014 water switch to the Flint River. She was aware of the river's toxic history. Yet Dr. Mona assumed Flint water was safe, based in part on a picture in her mind: trusted, hardworking government scientists in white lab coats stooped over test tubes and studying water quality. They were dedicated to protecting the health and safety of the public, she believed, just as she was dedicated to protecting children.

In late August 2015, as Flint residents amassed data and the Virginia Tech team found very high lead and more people died of Legionnaires', Dr. Mona invited two old high school friends and their families for a Sunday barbecue to celebrate summer's end. As the evening wore on, she wound up deep in conversation with her longtime pal Elin Betanzo, the valedictorian of their high school class while Dr. Mona had been the president.

Betanzo, too, had helped to shut down the town incinerator. She had gone on to become an environmental scientist and had worked for a time in the EPA's office of drinking water. Dr. Mona had never paid much attention to the details of her friend's work, in part because she didn't understand the technical jargon of water science. But on this night, Betanzo's quick, urgent tone got her attention.

Betanzo told her friend about an EPA water expert she knew, Miguel Del Toral, who had written an alarming memo about Flint water. Betanzo trusted Del Toral. If he wrote it, the document had to be true, which meant there was a serious drinking water problem in Flint. Betanzo continued with a crash course in water science, using some of those words Dr. Mona had never understood—corrosion control, distribution system, water main, service line, sampling, pre-flushing.

Lead.

"Lead in the water?" Dr. Mona asked.

She froze. She knew lead. All pediatricians knew lead. Lead came from paint or dust or soil. But water? No. That could not be. If true, it would mean that her tiniest, most vulnerable patients, many of whom already faced untold hardship, likely had been ingesting *over many months* a potent neurotoxin that could seriously damage their brains.

Dr. Mona returned, too, to those imaginary, trusted state water scientists in lab coats with test tubes, supposedly protecting public drinking water. Based on what her friend was telling her, these guardians of water were either grossly incompetent or liars. As she and others would later say, the environmental police were acting like environmental criminals. They had allowed a city to be poisoned and then covered it up.

And what about all those reassurances Dr. Mona had given

her patients? They had trusted her, and she had been unwittingly complicit. Betanzo asked whether Dr. Mona had access to blood lead data. All kids on Medicaid, which covered the bulk of Dr. Mona's patients, were required to be screened for lead at ages one and two. Couldn't Dr. Mona look up those results? Dr. Mona could show how lead in drinking water was leading to lead in Flint children, causing widespread harm. Dr. Mona could find the clear evidence, the absolute proof. She could do this, her friend urged. She had to try.

≋

On Monday morning Dr. Mona rocketed off to work. She contacted county and state health departments and the head of data at her hospital. And that week she saw her regular patients, this time through a new lens. Eight-year-old Brandon was having trouble focusing, and his teachers had noticed. Did he live in Flint? Yes. Did he drink tap water? Yes. In addition to screening for attention deficit issues, the doctor ordered a blood lead test and recommended bottled water.

Her next patient, Chanel, twelve, was obese and prediabetic. Chanel had lost ten pounds since their last meeting, and Dr. Mona offered a fist-bump for her success. She asked Chanel how she'd lost the weight. Had she cut down on sugary drinks, as the pediatrician had suggested at their last meeting?

Yes, Chanel said.

Was she drinking Flint tap water?

"Yes," Chanel said proudly. "Eight glasses a day."

The doctor's heart sank. She encouraged the family to drink bottled and ordered a blood lead test for Chanel.

Her next patient, fifteen-month-old Jasmine, was grumpy with a bad case of eczema that flared up after bathing, her mother said. Were they bathing in Flint water? Yes.

Could they stop?

How?

Dr. Mona suggested bottled water.

"You want me to bathe her in bottled water?"

Maybe they knew someone outside of Flint where they could bathe Jasmine.

"We don't have a car," Jasmine's mother said.

For the rest of the day, Dr. Mona focused on lead in water. She queried other doctors and medical students who saw more patients. Had they seen a rise in blood lead levels in kids? Yes, they answered: a one-year-old with a level of 7 micrograms per deciliter; two siblings with levels of 14 and 22. There was no safe level of lead in blood, Dr. Mona knew, though the government set an upper limit of 5.

For the next weeks in September 2015, Dr. Mona and a Hurley staff researcher gathered internal hospital data on blood lead levels in children. It showed a rise, but the sample was too small. They next tried and failed to collect more statistics from the county and state. Finally, with help from Dan Kildee, a Democratic US representative for the Flint area, the researchers acquired and analyzed 1,746 children's blood lead samples from the county. They ran the numbers, refining by age (under five), time period (to eliminate seasonal fluctuations, since lead levels rise in the summertime), by city and county (since county residents had continued on Great Lakes water), and by zip code within Flint, paying close attention to the areas with the highest levels of lead in water. They ran the numbers again and again, "a zillion times," Dr. Mona later said, trying to poke holes in their alarming results.

The data told the story: After the switch to the Flint River in April of 2014, lead in water found its way into the blood of children. Comparing the same seasonal periods before and after the switch, Dr. Mona found that the percentage of children in Flint under the age of five with elevated blood lead levels had more than doubled— from 2.4 to 4.9 percent. In two Flint neighborhoods, increased lead levels in children had more than tripled—from 4.9 to 15.7 percent in Ward Five, in the center of the city, and from 2.2 to 9.3 in Ward Six, directly to the west. Later research showed that the higher blood lead levels in children correlated with longer water stagnation periods in pipes, older houses, and poor housing conditions overall. Race proved to be a slightly less significant factor by neighborhood. Comparing Flint children with their "out-county" neighbors, however, did show racial disparity. The overall percentage of African American children outside of Flint is 24.4 percent, compared with the 76.8 percent rate of African American children in Flint neighborhoods with the highest water lead levels, Dr. Mona and her coresearchers found.

In all, some 27,000 children might be vulnerable to lead exposure in Flint.

Dr. Mona invited city officials to a meeting to share her findings, hoping to spur them to do something. Her allies at the meeting— heads of hospitals and health systems, a state senator, the head of the United Way of Genesee County—looked distressed, even tearful, knowing the potential harm to Flint kids. They spoke eloquently about acting at once to prevent further harm. But the mayor, Dayne Walling; the city overseer of water treatment, Howard Croft; and the city manager, Natasha Henderson, who still answered to the governor, remained apparently unmoved. That very morning, Walling said, they had met with state and federal regulators. "And they've told us there's no corrosion issue."

Dr. Mona spoke up. "This is a crisis," she said. "This is an emergency." The city needed to make an immediate change.

"That's impossible!" said Henderson, the state-appointed city manager. She said there were no corrosion issues. The water at the plant was fine, the officials implied. If there was corrosion in the pipes or people's homes, it wasn't their job to fix it. They would not be supporting Dr. Mona's disturbing findings.

Dr. Mona urged them to reconsider. This was an opportunity for city officials to stand with her as she shared her results and called for a health advisory. But whether they did or not, Dr. Mona and her team would be announcing the lead results publicly in three days.

That was a shame, said Walling. He had a scheduling conflict that day. He was meeting the new pope in Washington, DC.

Dr. Mona Hanna-Attisha announced her research findings at a September 2015 press conference after the city failed to act on her discovery and the state claimed her facts were incorrect. An investigation by the *Detroit Free Press* later confirmed her findings.

15

A Tipping Point

On a Thursday in late September, the five-foot-two Dr. Mona Hanna-Attisha, wearing her white doctor's coat and thick-rimmed glasses, peered out from behind a tall podium in a conference room at Hurley Children's Hospital. She could barely see above the bouquet of media microphones and computer screens. Five tall men who supported the doctor's findings stood like sentries nearby, from hospitals, health centers, and local community groups. Still, Dr. Mona was nervous. Moments before she had texted her friend Elin Betanzo: "I think I'm going to throw up."

People began to file in, including two stone-faced Flint officials who had been at Dr. Mona's presentation days earlier: Natasha Henderson, the city manager, and Howard Croft, of public works. Water activists appeared, as well as city council members, doctors, legislative aides, and many, many reporters with their crews and equipment. In all, about a hundred people filled the room. Mayor Walling was absent.

As cameras flashed and rolled, Dr. Mona launched the same PowerPoint she had presented earlier in the week. It began with a photo of an adorable one-year-old child, and Dr. Mona called her Makayla, a composite of several of Dr. Mona's patients to protect their privacy. Makayla had looked healthy and happy at her checkup, but a blood test revealed a lead level of 6. Since her birth, Makayla's mother had fed her powdered formula mixed with warm Flint tap water every day.

Like scientist Edwards earlier in the month, Dr. Mona had a prop—a baby bottle filled with Flint water. "This is what our babies are drinking for their first year of life," she said, holding the bottle up. "Lead-tainted water during the period of most critical brain development."

What would happen now to Makayla? Vast research showed she might suffer from lowered IQ, delays in speech or motor skills, decreased attention span, and more aggressive or violent behavior. And there were a host of medical ills Makayla could face in all systems of her body, from blood to bones to lungs, Dr. Mona said.

Speaking quickly and with nervous control, the doctor said the best way to help Flint children was to prevent lead exposure—by breastfeeding, avoiding tap water, using filters, declaring a health advisory, and, finally, reconnecting to Lake Huron water ASAP. "This research is concerning," she said. "These results are concerning. And when our national guiding organizations tell us primary prevention is the most important thing, and that lead poisoning is potentially irreversible, then we have to say something."

Among her audience, Melissa Mays, the activist parent who was familiar with all angles of the water crisis, sat at a table with her hand over her mouth, stricken by the new data. LeeAnne Walters shed tears. Curt Guyette, the ACLU reporter, felt the pivotal quality of the doctor's news. It was one thing to tell people that lead had polluted their water, but quite another to tell them the same lead now circulated in the blood of their children. And Dr. Mona's data, by comparing the before and after of the river switch, pointed directly at the changeover as the cause. Guyette saw a line of dominoes. Dr. Mona might have just provided the push to make them fall.

≋

The same day, the state denied the data and attacked the doctor. Speaking for the DEQ, Brad Wurfel sounded as if he were reading from an old press release when he said the water "is safe in that it's meeting state and federal standards." The same spokesman who had called Del Toral a "rogue employee" and accused activists of "fanning political flames irresponsibly" now attacked Dr. Mona's conclusions as "unfortunate." In the days that followed he said the water controversy had reached levels of "near hysteria."

A spokesman for the governor's office dismissed the research. Dr. Mona had "spliced and diced" her data. The state health department, which had refused to share its own data on children's blood lead levels, rejected the research and any connection between lead in children and the Flint River. The state health department had done its own study, bigger and better, and it showed no such lead increases in Flint children after the water switch.

A few days later, the director of the Michigan Department of Health and Human Services, Nick Lyon, ordered his staff to produce a report to suit his narrative, no matter what the data said.

"I would like to make a strong statement," Lyon wrote in an email to his staff, "with a demonstration of proof that the lead blood levels seen are not out of the ordinary and are attributable to seasonal fluctuations."

In Flint, City Manager Natasha Henderson refused to consider a switch back to Detroit water. It was "not something that is possible," Henderson said. "It's not a solution we can do at this time."

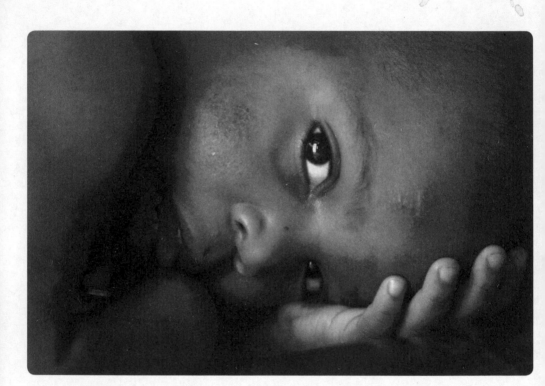

In January 2016 the sad-eyed image of Sincere Smith, his skin covered in rashes after bathing in contaminated Flint water, appeared on the cover of *Time* magazine. The photograph became a symbol of Flint's suffering.

16

A World Rocked

Following the doctor's press conference, Flint's deadly disaster surfaced like a beast rising from deep underwater, revealing its horrible dimensions to the rest of the world. Residents grew more alarmed—and utterly suspicious of what any official person had to say.

"Our government," the young amateur Flint singer Whitney Frierson thought when she heard the news, "the people who are supposed to help you are now trying to kill you, in all actuality."

Having ignored the story for nearly nine months, state and national media now pounced on Dr. Mona's findings and swarmed Flint, leaving residents both gratified and perplexed. Why the clamor now? *They* had been presenting experiential evidence and lamenting the untold harms of river water for nearly one-and-a-half years. Why hadn't anyone heard *their* voices? "I felt like, if you've ever seen that cartoon where your mouth is open and nothing is coming out and nobody can hear you," explained Reverend Bernadel Jefferson, reflecting on her experience after the news of Flint's water disaster had spread. "As we fought, as we spoke out, as we knocked on doors to let [residents] know that there was a problem, nobody would hear us. Nobody would pay us attention. [But] we didn't go away, and we didn't keep silent."

Now residents watched TV trucks with satellite saucers appear, stories and editorials multiply, and forgotten Flint move to center stage as Michigan's most ruined manufacturing town, outdoing even Detroit. The *Flint Journal* declared a "full-blown water emergency" and offered a novel idea: "There is a lake full of healthy drinking water just an hour away and the pipes already in place to bring it here," the editorial said. "Make the switch—now—before it's too late."

According to the new accounts, Flint was a catastrophe, a crime scene, an obscene failure of government. "If I lived in Flint, I'd be mad," said a *Detroit Free Press* editorial writer, Nancy Kaffer. "If I were a Flint parent, with a child who'd spent the last year and a half drinking lead-contaminated water, I'd be in despair."

The flood of news prompted moral outrage from near and far, and truckloads of aid to Flint suddenly contrasted with the months of heartless indifference of government. Water delivery rained on Flint: donated from local food banks, hospitals, and nonprofits. Flint churches held giveaways and ran through supplies in an hour. Students from neighboring towns held water drives for Flint schools, which soon shut down all drinking fountains and ordered students to bring bottled. The White Horse Tavern poured free drinks in exchange for water donations. The Saginaw Chippewa Indian Tribe gave. Uber drivers picked up water donations from Detroit and drove them to Flint daily. A jail in Flint switched to bottled for inmates.

Muslim organizations, Detroit churches, and union halls sent water. A nearby recreational vehicle dealer filled twenty RVs with water and drove them to Flint.

American generosity seemed boundless: a brewery in Cartersville, Georgia; school kids from Toledo; a radio station in St. Louis; the Elkhart Chamber of Commerce; the NAACP in Colorado Springs; church groups from Buffalo and Huntsville; a homeless shelter in Hartford; the city of Memphis; sororities and fraternities in Milwaukee; hockey fans from Ontario, Canada—all sent bottled water.

Entertainers and movie stars stepped in to save Flint, adding cultural caché to a crisis. Cher sent five semitrailers of water. Snoop Dogg, Eminem, Russell Simmons, Pearl Jam, Jack White, and Sean "Diddy" Combs sent water. Craigslist founder Craig Newmark started a crowdfunding page and said he would match every dollar with twenty of his own. Then Coca-Cola, Pepsi, Nestlé, and Walmart organized a truck lift: they delivered 6.5 million bottles of water to Flint. Later, Niko Goodrum, of the Detroit Tigers, delivered 1,400 bottles of water.

Millions of bottles. Distribution sites sprang up all over town and lines of domestic cars, trucks, and SUVs snaked for miles through Flint. Many arrived hours before the water hubs opened. Or people slept in their cars all night. For safe water.

Children who were old enough helped stockpile water. For some, it became an unpaid job. Ty Belin spent two summers collecting water. His brother drove a flatbed truck, and the two went from hub to hub picking up cases, then bringing them home and lugging

Gail Morton is moved by protesters gathering for a march to the Flint Water Plant. Some older residents said the protests reminded them of the civil rights movement. "We didn't even have the rights to live in certain neighborhoods," Morton said. "I am so proud today. I am really proud."

the cases to the basement, which came to look like floor-to-ceiling inventory for a water store.

At the Bethel United Methodist Church, a line of cars began at the pickup area in the church lot, stretched into the street, then snaked around two corners, down a highway, left again, and then for many more residential blocks to a dead-end street, where the line began to double back.

The overwhelming kindness was gratifying and urgently needed. Yet news of lead in children was not the end of a crisis but the start of awareness in Flint, as shock, panic, and rage set in. People began to speak of trauma. You could hear it in the words of Elder Sarah Bailey, who later described to a college classroom the many costs of the crisis. "This has impacted us from every angle you can think of," she said. "Our families, our finances, our housing, our economics—it has affected our health, it has affected our mental stability. I don't know about you but this thing took me into a place that I had to fight to get out of. I was angry, I was upset, I was depressed, and I was fighting mad."

Dr. Laura Carravallah was also shaken to her core. She was a pediatrician practicing at Hurley Medical Center and lived in a nearby town. As a member of the county medical society and a director on the county health department board she had learned all she could back in January when she'd heard about TTHMs in water. She had believed official reassurances about the water. Like Dr. Mona, she had trusted authorities.

"You start to realize after a little while that you trust in people and they may not be trustworthy," Carravallah told the same University of Michigan–Flint classroom, where she sat on a panel with Elder Bailey. "And that's a loss. That's a huge loss—to feel that your world is safe and then to start to feel that it's not safe. All of us, honestly, talked about having difficulty sleeping, of being sick to our stomach—not because of the lead, but because of this realization. Your whole world is rocked."

It was hard to capture the sense of ordinary life shattered in Flint. Yes, Flintstones lived with the known plagues of their city—all of those "worst of" designations of poverty, blight, and violence. Yet by September 2015 everyday life in Flint felt more profoundly dangerous. Many residents felt that their homes were no longer places of refuge or comfort; water was no longer a certainty; bathing was no longer as easy as the turn of a knob or lever; public officials were no longer trustworthy.

And residents found themselves revisiting every one of their health or behavioral twitches after April of 2014 from the perspective of tainted water. That it was nearly impossible to prove that bad water had caused bad health only worsened the sense of trauma. Dr. Carravallah thought with horror about her demonic coffee habit—all day, every day, carrying her cup of coffee. She boiled the water, which only intensified the concentration of lead, as Flint residents came to know. "I boiled and boiled and that hot pot probably has a crust of lead. I started to get terrible joint pains. I thought, 'Well, I'm getting older.' But I had joint pain in my upper body and hands and sometimes it was so bad that I had a hard time getting up out of my chair."

She went to a doctor for a checkup. Her blood pressure was high and again she told herself that she was aging, overweight, stressed. She began taking blood pressure medication. Another colleague from Hurley had a blood pressure spike and a gout attack. Those were symptoms of adult lead poisoning. Carravallah left her job and spent time at home in Davison, outside of Flint. Soon her blood pressure plunged and her joint pain disappeared. "I don't know if I was lead-poisoned," she told the crowd. "I can only surmise."

Much would remain forever a mystery. You could not necessarily trust a negative blood lead test. That only meant a person hadn't been exposed in the past thirty days. Blood lead testing was a drive-by, offering a snapshot in time. It could not tell whether a toddler had been exposed fourteen months earlier; in that case the lead would have already passed through the blood and lodged in the child's teeth, bones, or brain, undetectable in the blood. Like nuclear fallout, the true harm might not be known for years or decades.

Ronda Thornton blames the pain in her left shoulder and numbness in her fingers on toxic amounts of lead in her water, discovered after testing by Virginia Tech. "I've been so sick that I haven't been able to eat for months," she told a TV reporter in 2015.

Was Flint water the root of all maladies? In the absence of trust, the answer was yes. Sickened elders and dying neighbors; failing students and violent behavior; miscarriage, stillbirth, seizures, dementia, and skin rashes. Whitney Frierson sang at a funeral where a mother who drank tap water during her pregnancy lost her newborn twins. Studies show a pregnant mother can pass lead on to her fetus, leading to miscarriage, premature birth, low birth weights, and slow growth. Did bad water kill her babies?

Whitney's seven-year-old cousin couldn't count to ten or tie her shoes. Her grandmother's dementia had worsened and her seizures had increased. Whitney had spent the summer making Kool-Aid from tap water. She had become extremely ill with stomach pains and rashes all over her body. It had been the same with her cousin, who had broken out in rashes until her skin bled. Was it all the water?

Nayyirah Shariff, the activist, wound up in a Flint emergency room with symptoms of weakness, high fever, cough, and difficulty breathing. The hospital took chest X-rays. A pulmonologist remarked about her unusual symptoms and ordered breathing treatments with oxygen, steroid shots, and antibiotics. Her chart said she had a cold. "This doesn't feel right," Shariff thought.

She went home and called her brother, a nurse practitioner at a prestigious teaching hospital in California. She described her symptoms and medications. "That's the combination we give when it's pneumonia," he said. Later, when she visited her brother, she was diagnosed with pneumonia. She wonders whether she had Legionnaires' disease. She'll never know.

Throughout the crisis, Flint residents often took aim at Michigan governor Rick Snyder. After the release of a damning government report, the governor apologized to Flint.

17

Surrender

The young Dr. Mona Hanna-Attisha had hoped to present her find-ings at the Hurley press conference, step back, and let the numbers speak. She would watch someone important hit a switch to return Flint's water source to Lake Huron and Flint's crisis would van-ish. Instead, as state regulators disparaged her work and character, Dr. Mona went home and curled up in a ball on her bed. Maybe her numbers were wrong after all. She felt small and defeated. "I just told all of Flint to stop drinking the water and that all their children are being poisoned," she sobbed to her husband.

"You did the right thing," he reassured her. Like everyone else who had challenged Michigan authorities, she, too, would have to fend off the attacks and keep fighting.

Behind the scenes, EPA officials in Chicago discussed whether to dip into a special fund to provide more water filters for Flint. If they did, reasoned one, it might send the wrong message to other cities with old lead pipes and water problems. "I'm not so sure Flint is the kind of community we want to go out on a limb for," added another, in a comment that would echo beyond the casual email exchange for its callous, calculating, and, to some, racist overtones.

The State of Michigan remained impenetrable. The health department had refused for months to release data that would back up its claims. Now they held on to that data like a life jacket. They had deflected Flint pastors and Flint activists, city council members and state legislators, Virginia Tech scientists, and now Hurley research doctors. Flint was safe; its children were fine.

But small cracks began to appear in the state's fortress-like defense. The day after the press conference, the City of Flint issued a "health advisory" to citizens. The water was fine, the city reassured its citizens. The advisory was merely a "public awareness campaign" to let residents know that no amount of lead ingestion was safe.

≋

There was no doubt that the new media attention, though belated, exerted pressure upon authorities. The *Detroit Free Press* found a way to see the state children's lead data, the numbers the state had used to attack Dr. Mona's findings. The stunning results: the state's own numbers proved Dr. Mona was right. Despite a dip overall in state children's blood lead levels, Flint's had risen significantly with the switch to the Flint River. The upward trend, the newspaper noted, "should prompt state public health officials to examine a brewing public health crisis."

It was undeniable: the state had collected a set of facts to fit the story they wanted to tell. That story was a lie. The State of Michigan had lied. It had poisoned its own children.

Pressure on authorities intensified. Two days after the doctor's press conference, Nancy Kaffer, of the *Detroit Free Press,* aimed her column directly at the top. "It's hard to understand the resounding yawn that seems to have emanated from the governor's office, following news that an increasing percentage of Flint kids have been lead poisoned after a switch in the city's water supply," she wrote, adding that "it is Snyder who must come to Flint's rescue."

The local Fox News affiliate ran a story featuring suffering people like Ronda Thornton, a resident of Flint who had let Virginia Tech testers into her home in August only to receive an alarming notice in the mail. The letter explained that any blood lead level above 30 micrograms per deciliter was a sign of *serious* lead contamination. Thornton's was 138.

"I've been so sick that I haven't been able to eat for months," Thornton told the reporter. Thornton had been taking medicine in order to eat, and on camera she looked thin and sickly.

≈≈≈

On September 28 at Flint City Hall, residents returned to council chambers to speak at the regular city council meeting. Now that Dr. Mona's study supported the evidence citizens had been presenting for eighteen months, there was a sense of both vindication and fury. Ordinary citizens had predicted this horror and were proven correct. But there was no satisfaction in that because Flint's water was indeed toxic, and now the city's most vulnerable, its babies and young children, had been poisoned. There were almost *no words* to describe the depth of the sense of betrayal.

"Good evening," tried Nayyirah Shariff, with an audible sigh. She was dressed brightly in an orange print scarf and orange sweater over a yellow dress, and her words were equally bold.

"OK, the City of Flint has eroded the public trust and violated the social contract between the residents and their government," she continued, with applause from residents seated behind her. Borrowing from a contemporary political slogan that had become a popular sweatshirt in Flint, Shariff asked: "Do Flint lives matter?"

She set about answering her own question. Residents' anecdotal stories, personal medical records, and visual aids had been dismissed. "We were accused of making things up or being uninformed," Shariff said. Residents tapped a leading expert who discovered widespread lead in Flint water. "He was accused of grandstanding, being self-serving, and skewing the results," Shariff added. Dr. Mona's work had led to accusations that she had engaged in "splicing" of data, though her conclusions were finally corroborated by the state, after the newspaper exposé.

"So do Flint lives matter?" Shariff asked. "For the state and this administration, the answer is 'no.'" A state-directed fixation on short-term cost savings had resulted in a "crime against our community."

"What about the kids who have lead in their bloodstream?" she implored. "Or other illnesses that were exacerbated by this caustic water that is coming out of our taps?" The authorities had shown an utter lack of concern for the future of Flint's most vulnerable, their infants and children. But Flint's youngest were not "throwaway children." The lives of Flint youth mattered greatly.

Shariff called for an investigative hearing to discover the truth, and she made a final plea. "I also hope and wish and urge that we can be hooked up to Detroit as our drinking water source as soon as possible."

≋

As September rounded into October of 2015, the temperature was rising inside the state government. "High Importance" emails circulated, and the word "emergency" now came to the lips (or screens) of many. On September 30, Governor Snyder said: "In terms of a mistake, what I would say is we found there are probably things that weren't as fully understood when that switch was made." On October 1, Genesee County commissioners declared a public health emergency, urging all in Flint to use filters certified to remove lead, have their water tested by the city, and flush cold water through their taps for five minutes before drinking.

On October 2, the state held a press conference in a classroom on the grounds of Kettering University in Flint, where blue-and-white infographic signs rested on easels around a podium. "Taking Action on Flint Water," the signs said, outlining a ten-point plan to include providing free filters as well as water and blood lead tests. A cluster of bureaucrats filed into the room in front-office wear. The head of the state DEQ, Dan Wyant, defended his agency. He would later resign. The state medical director expressed concern for Flint children. Mayor Walling urged residents to "test, filter, and flush" their tap water. In the back of the room, Brad Wurfel, who had disparaged so many fact finders, apologized to Dr. Mona for calling her results "unfortunate." He, too, would later step down.

The state was admitting to a problem. Yet to some, the state's so-called action plan looked like *inaction* all dressed up. The only defensible solution was a return to Lake Huron water; anything less was unconscionable, Flint pastors said. Anything less amounted to more state failure, the *Flint Journal* wrote. "Do it," the newspaper urged. "Now."

Outside the press conference, about thirty protesters hadn't been let inside. Some, like Nayyirah Shariff, dressed in yellow hazardous materials suits and carried well-worn and hand-painted protest signs like "Not Your Lab Rats."

"I feel like we're in Hurricane Katrina. George Bush just flew over," said Pastor Allen Overton of the Coalition for Clean Water. "This is awful. We have a state of emergency here and they're treating it as though it's no real big deal."

Baby steps followed. The county health department declared a public health emergency. The state distributed 4,000 water filters. It hired and trained Flint residents and sent them door to door to attach faucet filters. But some residents weren't home, or wouldn't come to the door, or refused the service for their own reasons, denial among them. Many knew nothing of the crisis until the knock on the door. They had questions. Were the filters attached correctly? What did filters screen? Did they work? How often did the cartridge need changing? What if you forgot what the color-coding meant? What if you were color-blind? Or blind?

Stories proliferated, protests grew deafening, and celebrities called for the governor to be removed. Finally, on October 8, Governor Snyder announced that Flint's water source would switch back to Detroit. A week later, on October 16, the switch was made.

〰

In December, Flint declared an emergency. At the very end of the month, a task force appointed to investigate the disaster released early results that read like a failing report card written about a fourth grader with a bad attitude. The state's water protectors hadn't cared about safe water for people, but about doing the technical minimum to stay within the law. And their communication to the public throughout 2015 was marked by a "persistent tone of scorn and derision," the task force said. "The agency's response was often one of aggressive dismissal, belittlement, and attempts to discredit these efforts and the individuals involved." It added: "In fact, the MDEQ seems to have been more determined to discredit the work of others—who ultimately proved to be right—than to pursue its own oversight responsibility."

The next day the governor apologized: "I want the Flint community to know how very sorry I am that this has happened. And I want all Michigan citizens to know that we will learn from this experience, because Flint is not the only city that has an aging infrastructure." The next day Wyant, the DEQ head, and Wurfel, its spokesman, resigned. Maybe that would be the end of the story about Flint's troubled water.

Flint resident Tim Monahan tells his niece, Chadie, that he is too weak to give her a piggyback ride. Monahan, a survivor of Legionnaires' disease, still lacks the strength to work a full day in construction. "There are so many great people that are standing up and working on making this a better city," he said. "We're excited [by] that, but at the same time, you can't drink the water."

18

A Ceaseless Trail

The Flint water crisis, or man-made disaster, or government-led crime, consisted in a layering of overlapping timelines. There were the start and stop dates of the Flint River for drinking water, which correlated loosely with water and blood lead levels rising and falling. There were the timelines of community protest, of rogue scientific data released, of officials lying and then admitting the truth. Blame assessment started in late 2015. Criminal investigation, government hearings, and civil actions would start and drag on after that. The years-long work of lead pipe replacement developed its own start and stop chronology. And there was the immeasurable timeline of trauma. But the deadliest chronology of all surfaced for the public three months after the state admitted fault and switched back to the Great Lakes for Flint's drinking water.

In January of 2016, Governor Snyder declared a state of emergency, this one over Flint's outbreak of Legionnaires' disease, the one first recognized about a year and half earlier by local and state officials. It was when Tim Monahan, the carpenter and Legionnaires' victim, first learned that he was not alone but one of at least eighty-seven people sickened by the disease. Twelve people died— or at least twelve people died who had been clinically tested with a positive result.

Legionnaires' killed Odie Brown in January 2015; Bertie Marble in March; John Snyder in June; Nelda Hunt and Patricia Schaffer in July; Dwayne Nelson, Thomas Mulcahy, and Arthur Percy in August; and Robert Skidmore in December.

Some learned Legionnaires' had killed their loved one after the fact. That was true for the son of Debra Kidd of Burton, next to Flint. She was fifty-eight and in good health when one day in late July of 2014 she came down with a migraine headache and became increasingly ill. She died in early August. Doctors diagnosed Legionnaires'. But her son remained in the dark about his mother's Legionnaires' disease until the state declared the emergency, eighteen months after her death—after he went back to her doctors and asked.

There were likely others. An intrepid PBS *Frontline* team scoured death records over the eighteen months of the water switch, turning up 119 pneumonia deaths, a doubling of cases from the same period of the previous year. Experts said some were likely from Legionnaires', especially since the disease is misdiagnosed as pneumonia in about 40 percent of cases.

The disease outbreak led Carroll Kinkade, in retrospect, to wonder about her partner, Earl Woods, who also died in the summer of 2014. Kinkade remembers how Woods complained about his dry sinuses, and how in the early summer of 2014 he came up with his own home remedy—he moistened his nasal passages with tap water. He woke up in the morning, walked to the sink, leaned over the faucet, and sniffed water droplets into his nose.

In July the normally robust Woods wilted. Kinkade gently urged him to go to the doctor but knew not to tell the former marine what to do. One night in late July Kinkade got up and discovered Woods collapsed on the floor. She called an ambulance.

Woods had pneumonia, the hospital said. Kinkade spent the next ten days with her partner in intensive care until he died. Once the news of Legionnaires' was made public, Kinkade wondered. She had a gut feeling. She had never trusted Flint water. Now, to her last breath, she never will: "I will claim that water provoked Earl's death to my dying day."

≋

The friends and family of Jassmine McBride would also wonder. She was twenty-four in the summer of 2014 and living on Flint's north side with her mother, who had heard rumors the water might be unhealthy. She warned Jassmine not to drink it. But like many, Jassmine didn't heed the warning. She drank lots of water and bathed in it. She thought it was okay.

Jassmine had diabetes. She went for a checkup in August 2014, and doctors discovered her iron and oxygen levels were low and admitted her to the hospital. There, Jassmine's health worsened. Her mother, Jaqueline, received a call from doctors. "Do we have permission to resuscitate her?" they asked.

Jassmine spent two months in a coma. She regained consciousness with a weakened heart and damaged lungs and kidneys. Doctors told her she had Legionnaires' disease. "What's that?" Jassmine asked. She would become the youngest known victim of Legionnaires' in Flint.

In the months that followed, Jassmine was sedated and bedridden as doctors tried to control the infection. Through the help of physical therapy, she relearned how to eat and walk, with tubes coming out of her body. She began a regimen of dialysis following a diagnosis of kidney disease. During an October 2018 conference of environmental journalists in Flint, Jassmine and her mother spoke to reporters who stopped at the McBrides' small yellow house.

Jassmine, who walked with crutches and used an oxygen tank to breathe, described her struggle. "It was a real challenge to learn to breathe on your own and do dialysis, which wipes you out," Jassmine said. "Even with the breathing machine, I felt I couldn't breathe. I was afraid to lie down. It was a scary transition." She was unable to attend college but was taking online classes.

Reporters from *Frontline* kept up with Jassmine. They went with her to the doctor, where Jassmine invited doctors to attend her milestone thirtieth birthday party—July 2018. It would be a celebration of survival, with music, dancing, games, and a barbecue. Indeed, the party drew throngs of friends and family, and her cousin's dance team performed. Jassmine showed off a few dance moves without her oxygen tube.

Six months later Jassmine went to the emergency room short of breath. She lost consciousness. She died on February 12, 2019. The immediate cause was cardiac arrest, her doctor, Marcus Zervos, an infectious disease specialist at Detroit's Henry Ford Hospital, later said. "But she suffered from complications of Legionnaires' disease from 2014, which were kidney failure, heart failure, respiratory failure."

He added: "She was the story of Flint."

Volunteer Rick Hayood loads cases of water into cars at the Greater Holy Temple Church of God in Christ in October 2018. The site opened for distribution at 10 a.m., though residents began lining up in cars at 4 a.m.

A November 2018 rally in Detroit, organized by TV's Judge Greg Mathis, kicked off an all-day caravan that made stops in Pontiac and Saginaw to collect bottled water before arriving in Flint for distribution.

19

"A Gaggle of Bottled Waters"

In January 2016 the National Guard arrived in Flint, President Obama declared a federal emergency, and Ariana Hawk took her two young children to the closest elementary school in her neighborhood to have them tested for lead. She walked into the packed school gymnasium and took her place in a long line of anxious parents who tried to quiet their squirming children. A cadre of public health nurses pricked tender fingers for blood collection, and the gym echoed with little kids' wails and screams. Hawk, who was pregnant and had been drinking unadulterated Flint water throughout most of her pregnancy, felt scared and heartbroken by the scene. It was traumatic for her and for her children, and she was certain none of them would ever forget it.

Hawk met a reporter and photographer at the gym that day. She pointed to her two-year-old son, Sincere, and revealed the unexplained rash over much of his body, one he had had since summertime.

The photographer, Regina Boone, took pictures. A few days later, Sincere's image appeared on the cover of *Time* magazine: his small head resting on his palm, his cheek covered in a rough rash, his wide brown eyes gazing at the camera with a tender sadness. A photo caption said he was afraid of Flint water. It burned his skin. Sincere became the face of Flint.

Even so, some in Flint still did not know that poison swished out of their taps. In January 2016, when the uniformed National Guard visited some 33,000 Flint homes to deliver free water, filters, and testing kits, some residents didn't answer their doors, especially Flint's estimated one thousand undocumented immigrants, most from Central America and Mexico. Community leaders in those neighborhoods began distributing communications in Spanish.

The guard also staffed Flint's five fire stations for water distribution and nine other water sites around Flint. Soon, parts of Flint looked occupied.

Yet to know and see the crisis did not equal being free of it. It took an estimated eighteen months for Detroit water to replace the protective scale on the interior of Flint pipes. And Flint would now need an overhaul of its water infrastructure, or at least replacement of an estimated 45,000 underground lead service lines, the garden-hose-sized pipes that connected water mains running down the middle of the street to the hookups at every single house. That job would take years, in part because record-keeping for the location of lead service lines amounted to 45,000 ancient index cards stuffed in a file drawer, scrawled and smudged in pencil notations. In the meantime, Dr. Mona and Flint's newly elected mayor, Karen Weaver, said no one should drink the water straight. Even as lead levels dropped, residents still experienced discolored and smelly water, skin rashes, and hair loss. They were still taking their families to the homes of friends or relatives outside Flint to bathe once a week.

And for reasons that touched on both science and psychology, few in Flint believed tap water was safe to drink, no matter the government reading. Dr. Lawrence Reynolds, a pediatrician in Flint and a member of the state's advisory task force, said it was "irresponsible" to tell Flint residents that they no longer had to worry about the water. "Researchers can publish reports and say that the water is safe in 90 to 95 percent of households," Reynolds said. "In the medical field, we have to deal with the 5 to 10 percent where there is risk."

In the absence of certainty, Flint faced the daily drudgery of living without tap water. An average American uses from fifty to a hundred gallons of water a day for drinking, cooking, bathing, cleaning, and flushing the toilet. One pack of sixteen-ounce bottles of water holds about three gallons. Two cases of water would not stretch much beyond breakfast for a family of four.

The government had issued filters, but by some accounts, as many as half of the households in Flint did not have those installed correctly. And they were not certified to filter bacteria. County health officials said young children, pregnant women, and people with weakened immune systems ought to keep using bottled.

The new rules around water added layers of disruption, hassle, time. Ty Belin, the high school student living on Flint's north side, felt irritated watching water dribble through a filter in his kitchen sink. It took "freakin' forever." Once he captured that water, he poured it into a larger Brita-type pitcher with a filter. That process was even slower.

Ty's friend, Delante Mckenney, bemoaned the added time and

effort required to live safely day to day. "We've got all these tasks to do," said Mckenney, at sixteen. The crisis had started when he was eleven. "We've got to wake up at earlier times than what we would before—to boil the water. Get all of these bottles of water ready." He was speaking on the five-year anniversary of the disaster, when a panel of youths gathered to describe how the crisis had shaped their lives.

Another teen, Xavier Mitchell, said the crisis had turned bathing into a speed event. "You can't just get in the shower and settle down, [or] take a nice little bath. You can't do that. You've got to time your stuff," he told a local TV reporter. And even while Flint labored to replace every lead line in the city, there would be no quick fix for the loss of faith in government. "Even if they say it's safe to drink now, I'm still not going to drink out of the faucet," Mitchell added. "I'm going to get a bottle of water or boil the water. They've lied since 2014. I don't think they're going to tell the truth now."

Some people could afford the more elaborate trappings of clean water, with whole-house filters or private water delivery. They could replace their damaged dishwashers, water heaters, washing machines, lead fixtures, and indoor home plumbing, just to be safe. But many others could not. And so days of an upended life stretched into weeks, months, and years. After Ariana Hawk's son, Sincere, appeared on the cover of *Time*, the family moved out of Flint, which continued to shrink in population, a crisis all by itself. The photographer returned in May to see how Sincere was doing. New photos revealed that his skin had cleared and Sincere was no longer awake nights scratching. Meanwhile Hawk became a belated water warrior.

On the four-year anniversary of the crisis she staged a traffic shut-down on the local freeway. "Please help us," she called out on a car roof with a bullhorn. "We don't have water."

Even four years later in Flint, mile-long lines of cars waited for free cases of water. In October of 2018, a young Flint father work-ing the graveyard shift left his factory job before sunrise, picked up his young children, dropped them at school, and then took his place in the water line at the Bethel United Methodist Church on Ballenger Highway and took a nap. Hours later, he pulled up to a brigade of volunteers.

"Good morning," said Kaleka Lewis, a good-natured and vol-uble woman. "Would you like vegetables this morning?" The local food bank was by then offering fresh produce and other goods at water hubs.

"Yup," the driver said, leaning an arm out the window. Cool jazz guitar played from a robust sound system set up outside of the church.

"I have onions, squash, carrots, and cereal," Lewis said, and began placing vegetables in the back seat, adding, as she loaded a bag of onions, "would you like two?"

"Yeah, go ahead, since you insist," the driver said with a smile. "You wanna give me a bag of cereal, too?"

"If you insist," she said.

"What else you got for me?"

"Canned goods," Lewis answered, motioning him to drive for-ward, then beckoning the next car with a line borrowed from an old game show, *The Price Is Right*: "Come on down, you're the next contestant."

The previous driver called out: "My price was wrong?"

Lorenzo Lee Avery Jr. holds a case of bottled water while waiting for a car to pull up outside Flint City Hall during a Flint Lives Matter tailgating event.

Volunteers laughed. Water haulers up ahead continued loading cases into trunks.

The driver had a final message for Lewis: "Thank you for your kindness."

"You're welcome," Lewis said. "You have a good day."

"You too."

The late representative Elijah Cummings from Maryland, then the ranking Democrat on the committee, wondered how the nation would send Flint's children into the future. "Will we send them strong?" he bellowed. "Will we send them hopeful? Will we rob them of their destiny? Will we rob them of their dreams? NO! WE! WILL! NOT! DO! THAT!"

20

Blame without End

The truth of Flint's water disaster, once exposed, prompted new waves of moral outrage and demands for a reckoning. Who was at fault? And what did the Flint crisis say about the state of the nation? What did it mean that government at every level had failed Flint? Instead of doing their job of protecting people, the supposed guardians of public health and safety had blamed the victims, closed ranks, cheated tests, and disparaged citizens and denied them an elemental human need for survival, water. They had poisoned a city's children.

Throughout 2016 officials launched hearings, opened or concluded investigations, and put price tags and timelines on Flint's recovery. Lawyers sued the State of Michigan on behalf of Flint residents, and a settlement meant the state would pay to repair Flint's archaic system of water distribution, its rusted-out infrastructure. Activists, having helped to force the return to Detroit water, also sought accountability and reparations. How would Flint be made whole?

The Michigan Civil Rights Commission conducted hearings and issued a report. Much of the harm and hardship of the water crisis, the report concluded, had been caused by "structural and systemic discrimination and racism that have corroded your city, your institutions, and your water pipes, for generations."

And yet the polluted Flint River water had never, by itself, discriminated. To believe otherwise irked E. Yvonne Lewis: "There's this whole (misperception) that the only people affected by the Flint water crisis are poor, underserved, underprivileged, minority families," Lewis said. "But the water didn't decide that when it got to a person's house who had an education or a little bit of money, 'OK, I'm going to skip you.' What people do not get is that everybody was affected."

The visceral sense of outrage embedded in the Flint story—the sense that a horror like this should never happen to anyone in the US today—found some of its loudest voices in the halls of the US Congress during a fiery investigative hearing held during February and March of 2016 in Washington, DC. There the late representative Elijah Cummings, then the ranking member of the House Committee on Oversight and Reform, flayed key Michigan officials, refuted their hypocrisies, and used the full force of his probity and poetic and impassioned oratory to put the bureaucrats to shame.

On February 3, in a room packed with some 150 Flint residents who had traveled by bus to attend the hearing, Representative Cummings began in a quiet, reasoned voice. He spoke of the committee's moral obligation to investigate Flint. Michigan had failed its citizens, and now Congress was "the last line of defense." All levels of government would need to answer for their decisions.

Cummings reminded the hearing room about why they were there. "'Oh very young,'" he began, quoting a favorite song by Cat

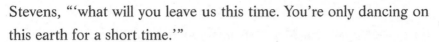

Stevens, "'what will you leave us this time. You're only dancing on this earth for a short time.'"

He continued in his own words: "I've often said that our children are our living messages to a future we will never see. The question is, what will they leave us, and how will we send them into that future? Will we send them strong? Will we send them hopeful? Will we rob them of their destiny? Will we rob them of their dreams?

"No!" Cummings shouted. "WE! WILL! NOT! DO! THAT!"

In March the committee reconvened. Committee staff had traveled to Flint to conduct interviews, and fifteen people had refused. One who did consent was former DEQ director Dan Wyant, who had shared "an interesting fact," Cummings reported. "In all the time he served as director, and despite all of the public outrage, the topic of Flint water was never raised in any cabinet meeting. "Not by Mr. Wyant, not by the governor, and not by anyone else. Ladies and gentlemen, there's something wrong with that picture."

Governor Rick Snyder takes his seat before a March 2016 hearing of the House Committee on Oversight and Reform in Washington. "Let me be blunt," Snyder said. "This was a failure of government at all levels."

Two days later Governor Snyder sat in the witness seat, his thin-by-comparison, Midwest-inflected voice a difficult match for Cummings's righteous baritone. Cummings explained how the House committee had collected documents showing that Snyder's closest staff knew about the Flint debacle from the earliest months following the switch. He ticked off their correspondence as proof, from a deputy legal adviser saying in October 2014 that Flint water was "an urgent matter to fix" to the governor's chief counsel warning the same day that "they should try to get back on the Detroit system as a stopgap ASAP before this thing gets too far out of control."

Dennis Muchmore, Governor Snyder's chief of staff, had also weighed in numerous times, concluding in one email, in February of 2015, "Since we're in charge we can hardly ignore the people of Flint. After all, if GM refuses to use the water in their plant and our own agencies are warning people not to drink it . . . we look pretty stupid hiding behind some financial statement." A few months later, in July, Muchmore said he believed Flint residents were "basically getting blown off by us."

Cummings paused between pieces of evidence to ask the governor to respond. In most cases Snyder said he did not recall or had no knowledge of the email or didn't remember specific conversations. He had arranged for fifteen hundred water filters to be delivered to Flint pastors, he said. He had understood only that Flint water contained E. coli and smelled and looked bad. His water specialists had told him repeatedly the water was safe, and clearly that had been wrong, he acknowledged. At other moments, Snyder blamed the EPA, asking why the Midwest regional head had never called him. "We needed urgency, we needed action, and they kept on talking," Snyder said.

Cummings was growing impatient. "OK," he said to Snyder,

"it looks like almost everyone knew about these problems except you. You were completely missing in action. That's not leadership." Cummings asked whether the governor could understand how Flint residents might not believe his denials, given that his closest aides were well aware.

"I absolutely do, sir, and I will have to live with this my entire life," Snyder said.

Cummings cut him off.

"You know, I have heard you say that, but I've got to tell you, there are *children* that have got to live with it—the damage that has been done—for the rest of *their* lives. And it is *painfully painful* to think that a child could be damaged until the day they die and that their destiny has been cut off and messed up. So, yeah, you have to live with it. But they—many of these children will never be what God intended them to be when they were born."

Further, Cummings pointed to the governor's written list of priorities, sent to staff in January of 2015. "Governor," Cummings said. "Flint water was not your first priority. It was not in the top ten, or in the top twenty, or even in the top thirty. Flint was number thirty-six. Shouldn't the children and residents of Flint have been higher on your priority list, Governor?"

And Cummings was incensed that the state carried a surplus throughout the crisis but used cost as a reason to stick with the river. Now the state was paying legal fees. "It makes me sick to think you found a way to have the State of Michigan pay more than one million dollars in legal fees," Cummings insisted, "yet you thought so little of the people in Flint that you could not be bothered to ask the state legislature for money to switch them over to clean water. You cannot be trusted and I gotta tell you, you need to resign."

A fellow congressman, Representative Matt Cartwright, a Republican, offered a similarly damning assessment.

"Governor Snyder, plausible deniability only works when it's plausible. And I'm not buying that you didn't know about any of this until October of 2015. You were not in a medically induced coma for a year. And I've had about enough of your false contrition and your phony apologies. [Regional EPA head] Susan Hedman bears not one-tenth of the responsibility of the State of Michigan and your administration, and she resigned. And there you are, dripping with guilt but drawing your paycheck, hiring lawyers at the expense of the people, and doing your dead level best to spread accountability to others and not being accountable. It's not appropriate.

"Pretty soon we will have men who strike their wives and say, 'I'm sorry, dear, but there were failures at all levels,'" said Cartwright, and some in the hearing room gasped at the analogy. "People who put dollars over the fundamental safety of the people do not belong in government, and you need to resign."

Former emergency manager Darnell Earley fared no better. Cummings asked Earley what he had been thinking when GM said Flint's water was eating its engines. It was the very same question the polite Carolyn Shannon had asked at a Flint City Council meeting more than a year earlier, and that citizens had asked in letters to the editor in the *Flint Journal*.

"Mr. Earley, I got to tell you, I almost vomited when I heard you say something a moment ago," Cummings said. "You said that even after you found out that newly manufactured parts were starting to rust out by using the Flint water, that you did not see that as a problem. I mean, wait a minute now, I am confused. If they are going to rust out newly manufactured parts, you mean that does not send you a warning that maybe human beings might be being harmed? Come on now!"

"Well, again," said Earley, who had faced a version of the same question minutes earlier. "I was relying on the information I was getting from the [Michigan water protectors] and from the staff. [. . .] I'm not a water treatment expert."

"You don't have to be a water treatment expert!" boomed Cummings. "A five-year-old could figure that out."

Frustration increased as blame shifted with each witness. "I think this hearing is going to be known as the Great Finger-Pointing Hearing," commented Representative John Mica, a Republican from Florida. "We've got [the] Flint mayor throwing people under the bus; we've got [the] Flint former emergency manager throwing people under the bus; we've got Ms. [Susan] Hedman, a former EPA administrator for that area, throwing people under the bus. But somewhere it seems like people were asleep at the top not doing their job."

In Michigan, as Governor Snyder was completing his term, the state attorney general filed criminal charges against three water officials for distorting Flint's lead results. Eventually fifteen state employees were charged, some for involuntary manslaughter in the Legionnaires' deaths. The web of blame required a map. Defendants in the criminal cases accused the attorney general of grandstanding— he had filed charges during his concurrent campaign for governor. The State of Michigan engaged a team of scientists to investigate the Legionnaires' source. The team soon came under attack from Marc Edwards, the Virginia Tech scientist who had helped to expose lead poisoning. Local activists, in turn, soured on Edwards after he began to assert that Flint water lead levels were dropping.

It was hard to follow the money behind every accusation and countercharge, especially the taxpayer money that went toward both prosecuting and defending Flint water cases. The state had hired a private lawyer to prosecute the criminal cases. But as it did for Governor Snyder, the state was also paying legal fees for the fifteen defendants—the people it had charged with crimes. And it was defending the same people against civil lawsuits brought by citizens of Flint for the harm done. Nearly six years after the water switch,

Protesters carry signs likening Michigan governor Rick Snyder to the devil as they await a scheduled march, with the Reverend Jesse Jackson, in February 2016. The march began at the Metropolitan Baptist Tabernacle church in Flint.

costs had climbed into the stratosphere. In one legal settlement, the state had agreed to pay $87 million to replace Flint's lead service lines. Flint schools in 2019 said the surging number of special education students would cost at least $3.6 million, which the district did not have. No one had tracked every dollar spent on the Flint disaster, but estimates of taxpayer costs had reached $600 million conservatively. Lawyers and an economist said Flint's costs, over time, could reach into the billions of dollars.

In the 2018 midterm elections, Michigan elected a new Democratic administration under Governor Gretchen Whitmer. Soon the new officials told Flint residents that the previous investigative work had failed to look at all the evidence. In June 2019, Attorney General Dana Nessel dropped all criminal charges. With thousands of new documents to examine, the team would start fresh. Once again, Flint felt dismissed and betrayed.

"How are you going to restore faith in institutions when nobody pays a price?" asked Benjamin Pauli, a Flint resident, assistant professor of social science at Kettering University, and author of *Flint Fights Back,* a book about the prodemocracy forces in Flint that helped expose the crisis. Pauli didn't know precisely who to blame or what punishment ought to be inflicted. There was a void.

"It's not good," he added. "It makes people feel like they truly don't matter. They won't be able to trust their institutions going forward."

State law gave prosecutors six years to charge public officials with misconduct in office. The sixth anniversary of the crisis would arrive in April 2020. Some Flint-area lawmakers had introduced legislation to extend the statute by another four years. Unless the deadline was extended, Nessel would have to race to refile charges. In late 2019 she set up a twenty-two-person office downtown, and by the time this book is published, new indictments may arise. The Supreme Court also cleared the way for residents to seek damages, ruling that government officials are not immune from civil actions.

On the five-year anniversary of the Flint water crisis, in April 2019, residents returned to the state capitol in Lansing to remind the world that Flint was still broken. They cited lead pipes remaining in the ground and a lack of criminal convictions.

21

"We Can Save Ourselves"

Even as lawyers filed, took back, and then promised new indictments, many in Flint had identified their own heroes and villains. Some blamed a few blundering people who failed at their jobs. In that telling Flint was rescued by a handful of saviors. Others pointed to a hundred years of racist decisions, the exit of General Motors, and a toxic legacy. In any scenario the final cost was incalculable: potentially thousands of vulnerable children faced water-related ills that could worsen over the course of their lives. And there was the ephemeral matter of trust, the binding thread of human interaction that had been shredded in Flint.

There were many candidates for villains: the smooth-talking mayor who pushed the button and drank river water on TV, twice; the stern emergency managers who hacked away at Flint's city services until there was almost nothing left, then raised any rate they could find—from water to sewer to street lights—in one of the poorest cities in the country. Many privately slung mud at the man behind the pipeline, the county drain commissioner, Jeffrey Wright. Or was it the slew of state officials—from emergency managers to the state treasurer to environmental regulators—who signed off on an invented "emergency" that allowed indebted Flint to borrow money from the state to buy into the pipeline? It was a deal that required use of the river for drinking water in order to pay for everything else.

A stand-out villain was the state law that wiped away the democratic process in Flint: the emergency manager law. It had left all local decision-making in the hands of a single person, a financier. Its very structure eliminated the normal checks and balances of government. Under the law, the state was policing its very own terrible decisions. "Everybody's on the same team," said Curt Guyette, the investigative reporter for the ACLU. "They're going to start covering up for each other."

The governor was villainous for pushing the emergency manager law and for his do-nothing, hands-off response to every warning sign in Flint. Mock wanted posters soon appeared on walls and light poles around the downtown Ann Arbor neighborhood where, in the midst of the crisis, he bought a loft condominium that many in Flint seemed to know cost $2 million. Chalk on the sidewalk outside his home read, "What Snyder did to Michigan children is criminal." Even five years later, chalk notes appeared outside his door. Harvard offered him a fellowship, but the outcry in Flint prompted him to refuse it, blaming the protest.

A villain was the national media, which ignored the story for too long and failed to act as a watchdog, believing government officials over the firsthand testimonials of ordinary people.

The State of Michigan, with its deadbeat bureaucrats at the

Department of Environmental Quality, had acted with staggering incompetence, according to the final report of the Flint Water Advisory Task Force issued in March 2016. "The Flint water crisis is a story of government failure, intransigence, unpreparedness, delay, inaction, and environmental injustice," it began. The state's department of environmental watchdogs had "failed in its fundamental responsibility to effectively enforce drinking water regulations." The state health department had also "failed to adequately and promptly act to protect public health." Both agencies had "stubbornly worked to discredit and dismiss others' attempts to bring the issues of unsafe water, lead contamination, and increased cases of Legionellosis [Legionnaires' disease] to light."

Or, as one Flint youth, sixteen-year-old Marquez Williams, assessed the official response to the water crisis: "I'd give the government a D-plus."

Who, then, were the heroes? Dropping in late to the story, the media latched on to a few: the whistleblower Miguel Del Toral from the EPA; scientist-mom LeeAnne Walters; Professor Marc Edwards of Virginia Tech; and Dr. Mona. In magazine and newspaper stories, the four appeared shoulder to shoulder, comrades in truth-seeking and telling.

Over time, the three experts and the citizen-scientist made media appearances, gave commencement addresses, published papers, and won grants and awards. A stay-at-home mom at the start, LeeAnne Walters was soon making speeches around the world. She won fourteen awards, including the prestigious Goldman Environmental Prize, the world's largest award given to grassroots environmental activists, with $200,000 in financial support. Her children use the pointy end of their favorite Smithsonian award—a representation of

Superman's Fortress of Solitude—as a lance for chasing each other around the house.

Edwards and Dr. Mona were listed among *Time* magazine's "100 Most Influential People" as well as its top ten "Person of the Year" finalists. Together they won the first-ever "Disobedience Award" from the MIT Media Lab. Dr. Mona wrote a book, weaving her role in the crisis together with her Iraqi American roots. Dr. Edwards won a $1.9 million EPA research grant to study lead in water.

But the limelight, accolades, and financial rewards for those few people made the activist residents of Flint feel, once again, left behind. It was not that the four were undeserving of recognition; they had been key. It was that the heart of the story had gone missing. The people of Flint had been left out. Even the so-called heroes said so.

"I think the credit mainly goes to the people," Miguel Del Toral later told an interviewer. "The people who are actually holding their government accountable. To the extent that we as public servants provide them with information and support—that we're paid to do—that's our role."

Walters agreed that everyone had played to their strengths: "We were an unstoppable force together as a team."

Much of the media had distorted the story by missing many months of activism, including the city hall meetings, the icy winter protests through downtown and outside city hall. They skipped the pastors going to Lansing, starting up water distribution sites, spreading the word. And the media jumped over the parts where Flint residents met weekly—preachers, activists, professors, parents—and furnished Virginia Tech with nearly three hundred water samples. They missed a story of citizen action that cut across race, class, religion, and party politics. In a highly segregated city in a highly divided country, Flint had demonstrated a spontaneous collective action that worked.

"What does it mean," asked Derrick Z. Jackson, a journalist and researcher who moderated the panel "Unheard Voices" at the annual environmental conference for journalists held in Flint in 2018, "for a story of this magnitude, in a city where the struggle was multicultural, that at the end of the day, no African-American figure in Flint was ever called a hero in the national media?" By portraying black residents, especially, as helpless victims, the media had failed to reveal their central, active role.

It was only after local concerns had been vetted by "elite" and mostly white experts that the media responded. The struggle itself had been multiracial; stories about the crisis revealed a "type of racism that appears in many forms all around us," Jackson wrote in a story on the missed black heroes of Flint.

At the same panel, Melissa Mays said the heroes were the people of Flint, the poor and the poisoned, the ones who came early to city hall or later marched in the cold or filed complaints or lawsuits or wrote letters to the editor or left Flint or returned and somehow carried on despite their expensive and tainted water.

And here was another takeaway from the disaster: that the people, under a law that thwarted the democratic process, still prevailed. Flint residents had fought, challenged the state, demanded better water, and finally captured the attention of the world. Flint was an example of the nation at its worst but also its best.

Curt Guyette, another panelist in the "Unheard Voices" talk, said no single person had exposed the Flint calamity; it was the sum of the whole. The so-called heroes had been crucial, each adding to the weight of evidence until it could no longer be denied. But the driving force had been the people of Flint. "A lot of people who were never before at the same table came together and worked together really effectively against long odds to eventually bring the crisis to the attention of the world," he said to reporters in the room. "And that gets missed an awful lot. It's just 'Oh, these people saved the city' when it was the residents who saved themselves. That's the really inspiring aspect of this story. The most inspiring aspect. And that gets lost. And that's unfortunate because it would help inspire other people to know we don't have to count on someone else to save us. We can save ourselves."

Flint resident Claire McClinton speaks at a June 2019 town hall–style meeting of the newly installed Michigan attorney general Dana Nessel. Nessel's office found fault with the first criminal investigation under her predecessor, Bill Schuette, and she dropped all original criminal charges. The new team promised Flint residents a more thorough and serious review.

22

Coming Back Where?

On a steamy Fourth of July morning in 2018, Ty Belin, fifteen, descends the steps of his family's two-story clapboard home on the north side of the city and turns left. He is walking downtown to meet friends. The sidewalk heaves and crumbles underfoot, so Ty veers across the median and into the street. He is annoyed by the treacherous sidewalk, tufted with unruly weeds at each crack. Why did the ground beneath Flint feel like one vast shattered, overgrown sidewalk?

Ty's street, East Dartmouth, looks lively enough, as it did when Flint was named one of the best places to live in America. That's when Buick City operated at the other end of the street. It was a massive car-making metropolis, some 165 football fields of General Motors manufacturing and the largest auto factory in the world, employing 28,000 people at its height. Now it looks like fields of

broken concrete. Chemical contaminants foul the ground under-
neath.

Ty heads west, into a ruined, dystopian streetscape that makes a
visitor want to gawk or cry. Here, on Flint's north side, thousands
of the remaining houses stand in states of wreckage: smashed
up, boarded up, caved in, blackened from arson fires. Around
the neighborhood, crews from the county land bank operate with
wrecking balls to tear down the dilapidated structures.

Since the departure of General Motors and the withering of Flint's tax base, thousands of
Flint homes remain vacant and abandoned, leading to illegal dumping, blight, and crime.
The city hired a coordinator to manage the problem.

Visitors call the scene "ruin porn" to mock their fascination.
Master planners call it a "green neighborhood," where parks and
gardens will one day flourish. Local residents see squalor or hope
in the wreckage, the death of a city or the rebirth of Flint. "They are
literally tearing down the hood," laments one north side youth. Ty
thinks it's looking a little better these days.

Lowell Junior High School in Flint sits abandoned and surrounded by debris. Twenty-two Flint schools have shut down, and some neighborhoods near the schools have become ghost towns after the closures.

Ty has come of age during the water crisis, and for him rotten water has faded into the background of everyday life. As Ty's friend Whitney Frierson has said, Flint water is "really just a cherry on top of all this stuff that happens in Flint, Michigan."

It was true that the water crisis had flattened Flint into a single story. And yet Flint is rich in dimension, a living showcase of American inequality, for one. Auto industry largesse had helped to build a fine cultural district that abuts a leafy, affluent neighborhood across from a working-class neighborhood of Latinx newcomers. A public housing complex sits on the outskirts, virtually cut off from Flint, while the Flint Golf Club hosts state PGA championships on the other side of town. Dollar, liquor, and phone stores line the streets while hundreds of immaculate churches stand in contrast to the blight. One young visitor tours Flint and calls it "devastating." A graduate student in public health, she has been studying Flint and understood that it was coming back. "Flint is coming back where?" she wonders aloud.

Flint's police blotter offers no good answer. Ty walks down Martin Luther King Boulevard, where an old brick structure is graffitied with "RIP Mike." A market farther down, D&H, is said to stand for "death and homicide."

Gun violence is killing Flint's children at alarming rates, especially its African American children. Flint's rate of gun deaths among youth is double that of Chicago's and nearly twice as high as Detroit's, according to the *Trace*, a national nonprofit news website that reports on gun violence. Yet shootings in Flint had become normalized, the sounds of gunfire a nighttime lullaby.

Victims could be the youngest innocents, like Zaniyah Burns, age seven, who was getting ready for bed in October 2018 when two bullets, no doubt intended for her uncle, flew through the window and killed her. "Long Live Zaniyah," read a T-shirt draped over a chain-link fence outside her home. "Forever Seven."

It was too much. People had grown numb. "I just want to see it change, man," said Aaron, a teenager, after the shooting death of his close friend. "Flint needs to be a better place. We've been taking too many losses. Too many mamas crying." Ty agrees; his friends agree. They can't even cry at funerals anymore.

Ty walks by Liquor Plus, a mini-mart painted a garish red and yellow with a history of arson and shootings. It was shut down once and the owner pled guilty to fraud. But it's open again—thankfully, to those who need it for food. Flint is a food desert. Residents rely on drug and dollar stores and gas station mini-marts for groceries. One north end liquor store sells a pork chop dinner with french fries and fried okra. A Michigan State University survey gave Liquor Plus a 31 out of 100 health score. Ty walks on by.

When residents leave Flint, people ask whether they've ever seen a shooting or a drug deal. It must be exciting, they say. When a professor of neurolinguistics took a job in Flint, her parents warned her to buy a taser. The stigma can be overwhelming. One young man from Flint found himself at a youth leadership conference in Detroit, where others from around the state were invited to write down words used to describe their cities on posters set up around the room. Flint's list grew long: GM, gangs, gun violence, emergency manager, corrupt government, poverty, poor school system, water crisis. The purpose was to let go of negative stigma, but the representative from Flint struggled. Most of the words were true, he thought to himself. "All of them, actually, are true."

At Flint City Hall, Sheldon A. Neeley, a former city councilman and state representative, defeated incumbent mayor Weaver in November 2019 and promised a new era of transparency and trust. But city council meetings had devolved into spectacles of dysfunction, and an audit showed continuing financial malaise in Flint, especially mounting costs related to pensions. Neeley promised to right Flint's ship.

You could paint Flint grim if you wanted. You could call it "Murdertown, USA," and you might not be wrong. You couldn't deny Flint's stigmas. But like the earliest versions of the water story, these were just the easiest truths.

Amber Hasan and Senegal Tuklor Williams, parents of six children, own an essential oils shop in Flint. Since the water switch, demand for a hair-growing product they sell has helped the couple establish their customer base. A growing number of local artists, artisans, and entrepreneurs are creating a homegrown renaissance in Flint. "We all have to use our 'thing'–whatever it is that we have–to make changes," said Amber.

23

Roaring Uphill

In her 2018 State of the City address, Flint mayor Karen Weaver described a city "roaring uphill." Across town, Angela Stamps, who runs a summer youth bike club at Berston Field House, uses riding a bicycle as a metaphor for kids: only you can push the pedals to move your life forward. There is an unmistakable civic propulsion in Flint. It is as if decades of hardship have culled the fragile flowers. The hardy, Flinty people remain, and they are passionate about progress, community, and the social good.

Carma Lewis is one of Flint's compulsive community builders. A native of the city, with brown skin, highlighted locs, and a radiant smile, Lewis is a connector of people, part of the hub of Flint's wheel. She cruises Flint in her stripped-down Jeep with a miniature baseball bat engraved with her name tucked under the front seat for self-defense. She stops to help out at water distribution sites, fields complaints and questions at city hall, and in between heads to Fish-land for her favorite fried catfish sandwich.

A nonstop volunteer, Lewis was working as a nonemergency dispatcher at the Flint Police Department when news of Flint's water crisis first broke nationwide. Her job turned into unofficial water dispatcher, directing U-Hauls and tractor trailers to intersections and parking lots around town.

After the crisis started, Lewis also birthed the community tool shed, an actual shed stocked with push and zero-turn lawnmowers, rakes, rototillers, and other yard implements. At the shed, residents are taught to operate the machinery, then schedule delivery of equipment to their homes, where they can mow like Iowa farmers—their lawn, their neighbor's, the tall lawns of abandoned properties. It was an all-around win.

Lewis says she's no activist—not even after the two years her family spent living without hot water after their water heater broke, corroded by lead. Then again, once they replaced it, Lewis kept the receipt. When Governor Snyder visited Flint, Lewis kindly handed it to him. A few weeks later the state commenced its water heater replacement program for low-income Flint residents.

It was difficult to see an upside to Flint's water disaster, but Lewis did. "I think Flint's more together than it was five years ago," she said, navigating her Jeep around holes in the road where pipes had been excavated or replaced. "New relationships have come out of this. It feels like it's in a better place." Still, Lewis only drinks her water filtered or bottled. "I just don't think I will ever drink water from a tap again," she said. "I think that part of my brain is broken."

≋

In the days surrounding the fifth anniversary of the water crisis, emotional rallies revealed the depths of anguish still present. Many who gathered—at the Flint Water Treatment Plant and on the steps of the capitol building in Lansing—carried old, familiar signs from years of water protest and wore new T-shirts: "Flint Is Still Broken." They carried a mock casket to remind the world of water deaths. And they lit and launched lanterns into the sky for those who had died, known and unknown. In Lansing, the state capital, a three-year-old sat on her mother's lap. She had been lead poisoned as a baby, and now she was small for her age.

A few days later at a union hall in Flint—the very birthplace of the United Automobile Workers—lawyers for aggrieved residents offered a sense that Flint's struggle was once again resonating beyond its borders. Class action suits were heading closer to settlement or trial, and along the way Flint was plowing new legal ground, according to Michael Pitt, coleader of the civil cases. "These decisions are historic," Pitt told the union hall crowd. "These decisions are being cited by other lawyers" in similar claims around the country, he added. "Cities around Michigan and throughout the country are testing the lead in their water and finding dangerous levels, all because of the example set by Flint."

If you highlighted the best of Flint's response to its crisis, you could share best practices with every other similarly suffering town or city with lead in the water. Because like other moments in Flint history, the city's water crisis is a portent for the nation. "America is a thousand Flints," wrote one Buick historian in 1945.

Andrew Highsmith, author of *Demolition Means Progress*, the social history of Flint, writes that the nation is still made up of a thousand Flints, but they are the thousand plagued by economic depression, hypersegregation, and suburban surrounds that reinforce social inequality.

Infrastructure, too—the built environment that helps to organize American community life—is falling apart. The latest report card by the American Society of Civil Engineers on American infrastructure—the schools, roads, bridges, phone lines, water and sewage treatment plants, and power generators—gave the nation a D-plus rating.

In addition to crumbling public works, research has shown a new variety of socioeconomic segregation: environmental injustice, or the deepening disparity between the effects of environmental crises on the poor versus the rich. And in the US, the economic divide was growing deeper and wider. When economic austerity was added to that mix, it was a recipe for more Flints.

Already there were signs. In July 2019, California's water regulators described a lurking tap water crisis in the state. They identified 1,000 community water systems that may be at high risk of failing to deliver potable water—one out of every three. The troubled districts echo Flint, often falling within poor areas with small budgets, and they lacked the means to fix or replace their old water systems. In one small community, Willowbrook, near Compton in Southern California, residents had complained for more than a year about discolored, smelly water gushing from their taps and skin irritations that led to intense scratching and scars. Los Angeles County took over the small district, which lacked the money to fix its collapsing infrastructure.

In early 2019, Denmark, South Carolina, drew Flint residents to its protests after the small southern town learned its water system was tainted. Contaminants included cancer-causing dry-cleaning chemicals and an excess of manganese, which is benign in small amounts, but when inhaled in large concentrations has been linked to a condition similar to Parkinson's disease. More recent studies have shown a link to developmental problems in children. Denmark's well water had also been treated with HaloSan, a chemical that had not been approved by the EPA.

≋

And then in 2019 came Newark, New Jersey, with its uncanny parallels to Flint, like the frightful return of a monster from the deep. Newark had been assuring its 285,000 residents for more than a year that their drinking water was "absolutely safe," according to a city website. When testers learned otherwise, in late 2018, they began an urgent giveaway of 40,000 filters to residents. Then, in August 2019, testers discovered the filters had failed to properly remove lead.

Suddenly, in ninety-degree heat and oppressive humidity, people in Newark were standing in water lines to receive their inadequate one or two cases of bottled water—just like in Flint. Suddenly Newark residents were uttering the same words as Flint residents: "At this point I don't trust this administration at all," Rasheeda Scott, thirty-four, told a reporter from her Newark front stoop. "They've just denied, denied, denied there was any problem—but look now."

In response, Flint mayor Weaver issued a statement that she was devastated to see another community turn to bottled water due to lead contamination. She urged the country to replace moldering infrastructure before other people were harmed: "We knew that

Flint was not the only place facing such a crisis," she added in a press release. "We were just the most publicized, and we warned against the dangers of not dealing with failing and aging infrastructure all over the country."

The lessons of Flint were also imparted by documentary filmmaker Michael Moore, a Flint native who chronicled the city's abandonment by General Motors in his 1989 film, *Roger & Me*. As Newark reeled, Moore appeared on a late-night cable-news talk show with free advice for Newark's distressed residents. Do not imagine, he said, that you can wait patiently for your water to be fixed.

Just like Curt Guyette of the Michigan ACLU, Moore saw a lesson in Flint for the rest of the world. "I'm telling you right now," said Moore, wearing his signature baseball cap, "if you are waiting for the State of New Jersey, for the City of Newark, for the National Guard, for anybody to come and save you, let me remind you that you live in Newark."

Sharp racial and economic divides across the US meant that wealthy white people in Bedminster, New Jersey, or Grosse Pointe, Michigan, would likely never face hours-long waits in the hot sun to receive two cases of bottled water. But Newark—larger, growing, and in other ways distinctively different from Flint—was still a majority-minority city with a higher rate of poverty than the national average, with older housing stock, lead plumbing, and an industrial past. Newark residents, like Flint's, did not necessarily fill the campaign coffers of elected officials. They did not pull the levers of power like the big drug, gun, or tech lobbies. They could not phone the White House one afternoon and insist on, say, new funding for infrastructure.

Certainly other Americans, as in Flint, would feel the injustice and come to Newark's aid. Celebrities would likely dispatch truck-loads of water. Political candidates might pass through and say the right things. But it was Newark's voices, like Flint's, that together would need to form their own massive chorus and roar. "You're not going to get help in Newark unless you demand it," said Moore, "unless you fight for it, unless you rise up, nonviolently, and say, 'We cannot live like this!'"

Roaring uphill could be a subtle thing. And the roar heard by one person might sound like silence to another. There were signs of renewal in Flint. The old Capitol Theater shines in primary colors after a $37 million renovation, the most expensive in Michigan. The gussied-up Flint Farmers' Market is a hub of artisanal produce stalls and ethnic restaurants. Near the market looms the well-landscaped campus of the University of Michigan–Flint. Flint boasts four colleges and universities.

Major investors have bought historic buildings downtown and converted them into startup offices and common spaces for entrepreneurs. There are hipster coffee shops and an independent bookstore, Totem Books, which hosts Drag Queen Bingo night once a year. From certain angles downtown Flint has a Brooklyn vibe. Some see the evils of gentrification while others focus on the roar uphill.

Meanwhile, a maker culture, a rising group of young artisans and entrepreneurs, has caught on in Flint. The sons and daughters of auto workers are turning artistry and craftsmanship into money-making ventures. One hub is Factory Two, a century-old building that began as the Dort Motor Car Company, maker of horse-drawn carriages and then cars. Since the water crisis, the factory has been converted into a maker space with wood and metal shops as well as the tools and equipment needed by emerging artists, musicians, jewelers, clothiers, and more. Flint has a rich history of making all sorts of things, not just cars. It's in Flint's blood.

"People really try to make us hate our city," says Sara Johnson, founder of Girls Rock Flint, a program that brings adolescent girls together around music. "But I love it here and I know so many other people who do." Johnson is featured in *Forged in Flint*, a seven-minute film that highlights the growing maker culture.

Kiara Tyler started a clothing line, Kalm, whose bold graphic tracksuits are spotted on young black celebrities around the country. Tim Goodrich is a pastor-turned-shoemaker who sells his handmade leather boots, a pair of which showed up on actor Kevin Bacon's feet. Keysa Smith, who grew up on the north side of Flint, landed a four-year sentence in federal prison. Once released, she invented Spectacular Spudz, a lively food booth at the Flint Farmers' Market that offers mountain-size meals, starting with a baked potato.

Around the corner from the farmers' market is the eponymous Tony Vu at MaMang, a Vietnamese restaurant specializing in pho, the classic noodle soup. Vu was a drummer whose musical friends had turned to heroin. He turned to food. "You can have an idea here and make it into reality," Vu said. He started with a food truck on a whim. Six years later he has three restaurants and is about to move into a brick-and-mortar downtown location. "I don't know where else that can happen in the world," he said.

And Oaklin Mixon started GoodBoy Clothing, a business with a mission. Mixon was a foster care kid in Flint and fell in love with his city. He decided to use his skills to build a business "here in a place that actually needs it versus leaving it." His industrial-chic store-front shop features stacks of cool T-shirts, bow ties, caps, shoes, and sunglasses. His production room in the back is filled with sewing machines and printing screens. Everything is made in-house, and the store's guiding philosophy is painted on the wall: "We are a group of culture architects," it says, who want to "artistically express that we as individuals are leaders rebuilding the ruins of our cities and culture. We are tailored for the good of all."

Mixon, who closes *Forged in Flint*, radiates the young, organically grown, and forward-looking entrepreneurs of Flint. "The city that fell down and was able to get back up—that's Flint, baby. We got that grit. You can't just tell us no. You can't tell us no here. We're going to get to yes somehow."

Keishaun Wade views the Flint water crisis as an extension of Flint's history of extreme racial segregation and discrimination. He received a full scholarship to Cornell University after graduating from Southwestern Classical Academy.

24

"My Destiny Is Dismal"

To Keishaun Wade, the student at Southwestern Classical Academy, the road to yes was not at all clear. When he enrolled in Flint schools after his grandmother died, he had little faith in the future, just as the morning security drill at his high school suggested limited faith in Flint students.

Statistically, too, Keishaun had almost no hope of success. As a homeless child held back in kindergarten and the son of uneducated teen parents, he was likely doomed. Doomed to miss college and doomed to poverty, if the data were true. "My destiny is dismal," he wrote in a college essay. He had spent his life searching for comfort and safety. Without it, he knew, "hurt can harden you and follow you."

Yet his sense of doom was his place of inspiration. Keishaun was an authority on poverty, homelessness, violence, broken schools, toxic water, and bottomless mistrust—all inspiring his hunger for change. It must've shown, since he was elected president of his junior class at Southwestern. His intellectual gifts led him to join the Quiz Bowl, the Science Bowl, the National Honor Society, and the chess club. He ran track. He and his brother, Kwame, visited Flint Soup, a nonprofit that offered microgrants to budding entrepreneurs—a Flint version of TV's *Shark Tank*—where you put your $5 donation in the "taco bowl of destiny" and then made your pitch. Keishaun and his classmates lobbied the school board for proper heat, and Keishaun worked with a national environmental group to test Southwestern's water quality, which showed "crazy high amounts of lead."

His friends at Flint Soup knew of a national youth award that seemed to fit Keishaun Wade. In the spring of 2018 Yale University bestowed the Yale Bassett Award for Community Engagement upon Keishaun and fourteen other high school students across the country. He was flown to Yale, recognized in a ceremony, and introduced to a law professor, James Forman Jr., who had just won a Pulitzer Prize for his book on mass incarceration, *Locking Up Our Own: Crime and Punishment in Black America*. Forman inscribed a copy to Keishaun, who said it was the best book he'd read in a long time. He dared to wonder: Would Yale ever admit a formerly homeless kid from a broken-down, poisoned town like Flint?

≈≈≈

He applied to seventeen colleges and prayed for Yale. He knew the exact moment when the news would arrive, and he stared at his email inbox and counted down. When the news came it was disappointing: Yale was a no. Keishaun carried on. He pushed through his last months of high school and finished his senior thesis on education and urban decay. Soon more college letters poured in, a mountain of yeses: from Massachusetts, Maryland, Michigan, Georgia, and finally from Cornell, which offered him a place in the class of 2023 with a full scholarship. Next to Yale, it was Keishaun's unquestionable next choice. He posted the news and received hundreds of likes, loves, and exploding emojis of congratulation. Later, he shared a post on fighting "impostor syndrome," the sense that you've arrived at the place you longed to be only to feel that you don't belong. It's a lie, the post says. "You're capable, you're allowed to learn, you belong."

In June he landed in Ithaca, which might as well have been the place in Greek mythology for its strangeness to Keishaun. He bonded with the admissions officer and got to know some classmates. Their eyes went wide when he named his hometown. They had questions. His English professor asked if he might like to teach a class on Flint. Keishaun said he would. He would not sugarcoat the hardship. He would speak of structural racism and microaggressions and poverty and violence and betrayal. But then he'd talk about the friends who had started businesses during high school: in modeling, hairstyling, T-shirt design, eyelash sales, and graphic and computer design. He would describe Flint Soup and the microgrant he and his brother had won to start Supreme Lawn Care—to mow lawns and help fight Flint blight. And he would convey to his Cornell classmates the verve and drive—the unmistakable uphill roar—of Flint. "There are so many dope people in Flint," he would say. "The people, the culture; it's very unique. Anyone else would be despairing. But people in Flint thrive."

When musical composer Andrea Ramsey was asked to write a song for a choral fundraiser, she turned to the Flint water crisis. Searching for relevant lyrics, Ramsey discovered a poem from the 1800s with resonance for Flint today. But the poem, "Flint," by Christina Rossetti, was too short. To lengthen it, Ramsey sought out choir students from in and around Flint to add their words to the lyrics. "I wanted it to be honest," Ramsey said of the Flint piece, "but I wanted mostly to provide the city with exposure and to open the eyes of others to this massive, ongoing tragedy." The result, a choral piece that tells a story of Flint water, has been sung by at least twenty-five choirs around the country. Many are viewable on YouTube; the sheet music is available at sheetmusicdirect.com.

BUT A FLINT HOLDS FIRE

An emerald is as green as grass;
A ruby red as blood;
A sapphire shines as blue as heaven;
A flint lies in the mud.
A diamond is a brilliant stone,
To catch the world's desire;
An opal holds a fiery spark;
But a flint holds fire.

    The water started to change color. It was a
    murky white color.
The water was brown. It was a bright yellow color.
    My water had orange little pieces in it.
The water
We can't use the water.
    In school, they shut off all the water fountains.
We can't use the water anymore.
    My siblings and I were all tested for lead
    poisoning. A week passes and my mom
    finds out that all four of her kids have lead
    poisoning, including the baby. My mom and

dad were angry. I didn't want to believe it was true.

We all have to get tested.

There's no cure for lead poisoning.

We didn't know.

During the time the news was telling people not to drink the water, my family didn't have cable or internet, so we didn't know. We had no other choice but to drink the water.

We didn't know.

Flint is in a rocky place right now. Who can we hold accountable for this? We have to do everything with bottles and jugs of water. I constantly fear running out of water.

A flint lies in the mud.

This is our home.

A diamond is a brilliant stone to catch the world's desire.

An opal holds a fiery spark.

But a flint holds fire.

I still have faith in Flint. There are so many promising people here, there are respectful and wise people. There are beautiful neighborhoods.

A flint holds fire.

People see us as a bad city, but Flint is not bad. Flint is not trash. We are often overlooked and underestimated, but we are powerful.

We are powerful.

    We have kind people who help each other.

We are strong together. This is our home. We are
    powerful.

    No matter how deep and dark the mud is, the
    people in Flint hold true and bright.

We are powerful.

    No one should feel alone in times like this.

We are powerful.

    I sincerely hope that Flint has a brighter future
    ahead of it.

—Choral piece by Andrea Ramsey,
    based on writings by Flint children and
    Christina Rossetti's poem "Flint"

More than 5,000 water bottles rain down on a spring performance by University of Michigan–Flint student dancers. The performers collected the bottles they used during weeks of rehearsals for the event. One way to recycle Flint's water bottles has been to use them as a medium for visual and performing artists.

A Note from the Authors

I have had the good fortune to speak at MAME—the Michigan Association for Media in Education—several times. And whenever I go I get a chance to catch up with Cindy Dobrez and Lynn Rutan, who have been chairs of ALA Best Books committees, are the cocreators of the Bookends Blog site, and generally know books for younger readers as well as or better than anyone else in the country.

I think it was at one of those conferences, or shortly after, when Lynn said that we really needed a book about Flint and the water crisis. I knew that she was right: Flint is an X-ray of this country now, and one that must be shared. Yet I also knew that I am not the skilled reporter, the on-the-ground researcher who could do the story justice. And time mattered—it would take the better part of two years to do the research and writing, and then to bring the book to the world—and in today's news-cycle world, a story everyone is gripped by today can be forgotten by tomorrow.

I needed a coauthor, a person who was a skilled researcher and reporter, who knew Flint and Michigan, their history and politics, who had the time and motivation to make many trips to Flint, and who could write for a readership that would demand to be engaged on every page. Marina Budhos, my wife and sometime coauthor, suggested Candy J. Cooper—a writer she knew who, while a reporter at the *Detroit Free Press*, had been part of an award-winning team covering the plight of Michigan youth. She had also been a finalist for a Pulitzer Prize as a reporter in San Francisco. Now she was working for a nonprofit tutoring organization whose mission is to provide educational help to kids in need in order to close the achievement gap. I asked Candy if she would like to be involved; I didn't have to ask twice.

—Marc Aronson

≈≈≈

I was sitting in a midtown sandwich shop in New York City with my oldest friend from junior high school when I came across a brief note from Marc Aronson, whom I knew through his wife, Marina Budhos, a distinguished author of both fiction and nonfiction. The moment I read Marc's note, I had a visceral sense of something clicking. "Wonderful idea," I wrote back. "This resonates."

That resonance was soon fortified by my every dive into the Flint story. Whether it was at the end of a phone call, after reading the latest newspaper story, or reviewing video or audio recordings, I came away in those early research days nearly shaking. "I can't believe this!!!" I'd roar to the closest soul.

I think what bothered me most was how the lived experience of Flint's residents was either ignored, minimized, or mocked. The more vivid their descriptions of the water and its harms, the more outraged I felt: houseplants, gardens, lawns, and pets withering; children hurting and poisoned; people hospitalized; and, ultimately, people dying. It seemed Flint was drinking one kind of water, laced with heavy metals and bacteria, and officialdom was drinking another—a potion that made them oblivious. Author C.S. Lewis wrote that the roots of evil are not found among hardened criminals or even death camps, which are the end result. He said it is "conceived and ordered (moved, seconded, carried, and minuted) in clean, carpeted, warmed, and well-lighted offices, by quiet men with white collars and cut fingernails and smooth-shaven cheeks who do not need to raise their voice."

I started my research on Flint in 2017, at about the time a wave of assessments surfaced about what had gone wrong. Coming late to the story, I had the benefit of criminal complaints, task force reports, transcripts of hearings, a twelve-session course offered by the University of Michigan–Flint on the water crisis—recorded and available as a video on YouTube. Then came a vast number of research papers studying everything from the water crisis as a public relations disaster to the mental health consequences, youth perceptions, and effects on maternal outcomes. Some research faulted the first takes on the story, asserting that it only became a story after white people said it was so. Another paper argued about the proper adjectives to use about Flint, asserting that Flint children should not be described as "poisoned by" but only "exposed to" lead, which drew criticism.

The closest reporter to the water crisis, or the one who has written the greatest number of newspaper column inches, must be Ron Fonger of the *Flint Journal*, whose daily coverage serves as a solid and thorough first draft of Flint water crisis history. Photographer Jake May, also of the *Journal*, has been one of its chief photographers, enhancing the story with artful images that convey not only news but human emotion, a great help to those not there in real time.

Soon books on Flint began to appear, and I benefited greatly by scouring those with my neon highlighters and Post-it Notes. *Poison on Tap* was a timeline and collection of stories produced by the staff of *Bridge Magazine*, a nonprofit statewide news organization in Michigan that included some of my former colleagues. Dr. Mona Hanna-Attisha's memoir, *What the Eyes Don't See*, focused on her discovery of blood lead levels in children and how her Iraqi American upbringing prepared her for her public health crusade in Flint. Detroit journalist Anna Clark's *The Poisoned City* came next, and it is a thorough and affecting book about how the crisis unfolded and what went wrong. After these came social scientist and Flint resident Ben Pauli's 2019 *Flint Fights Back*, a close and nuanced analysis of Flint residents working together to expose the water crisis as an environmental injustice.

An earlier academic book, written before the water crisis broke and published in 2015, informs many of the later articles and accounts. *Demolition Means Progress*, by Andrew Highsmith, offers a detailed social history of Flint and reveals the many historical forces that made it the most segregated northern metropolis in the country. If Highsmith had set out to write a prequel to the water crisis he could not have done a better job. The book became a kind of bible in Flint. Study groups met with the author, now a professor of history at the University of California–Irvine, for talks on specific chapters. The state civil rights commission report on Flint relied heavily on Highsmith. Keishaun Wade read it and discovered sharp parallels to his own life.

I added older and newer volumes to the collection above. There was *Stereo(TYPE)*, a raw and powerful collection of poetry and prose by Flint-born poet Jonah Mixon-Webster, who won the 2019 PEN/Joyce Osterweil Award for Poetry. A section of his book concerns the water crisis.

In stark contrast, one day in Totem Books I came across *Picture History of Flint: The Flint Journal Centennial*, published in 1975 and featuring glorious Flint moments, like the huge downtown parade in 1954, known as the Golden Carnival, celebrating the making of General Motors's fifty-millionth car, which was gold-plated. Or the parade the following year, which drew 200,000 people downtown and featured a float with the actress and singer Dinah Shore, who sang the jingle "See the USA in your Chevrolet."

That book also reminded me of Flint's segregated past, not only because most every photograph featured white people. One photograph captured hundreds of hooded figures on a grassy hillside, and the caption identified the image as that of the Ku Klux Klan state convention at Flint's Kearsley Park in 1927.

While perusing the photo book at home, a loose yellowed clipping fell out, a full page from the September 2, 1979, *Flint Journal* about the demolition of an architecturally unique downtown building on the Flint River. The photos in the article showcased the Romanesque archways, ornamental tile work, and cut-stone framing of the 1925 Commerce Building. It was to be knocked down, the story said, to make way for a Hyatt Regency Hotel and convention center, envisioned as an answer to factory closings. The swank hotel would attract tourists to Flint, while a new downtown amusement park, AutoWorld, would similarly draw out-of-towners, the city planners reasoned. But the tourists never came, and AutoWorld and the Hyatt became Flint's most infamous redevelopment flops. The Hyatt building, today an ornamental void of brick and glass, was passed along to other owners and finally donated to student housing.

I couldn't help thinking about the racial overtones of that plan. An old TV ad for the new Hyatt features a white couple drinking and dancing intimately, with the woman finally looking into the camera with a beckoning whisper: "Come on." Were Flint's redevelopment plans in the 1970s made with input from residents, or even with the idea of attracting a diverse group of residents and nonresidents? It didn't appear so, likely a fatal flaw.

My first trips to Flint challenged my sense that I was somehow meant to write about it. By the time I arrived the city had grown suspicious of out-of-town journalists and researchers. There was a feeling, as Elder Sarah Bailey had said early on, that people came and went without considering the footprint they left behind. She would later say that each new wave of researchers seemed to pick at Flint's scab, at the trauma of the water crisis, and that no healing could take place until that part was over. And Flint needed to heal.

I had first run across Flint's outsider fatigue after an old, close friend from my earlier newspaper life put me in touch with her good friend from her previous newspaper life now living in Flint, Jan Worth-Nelson, a poet and editor of the local monthly *East Village Magazine*. I wrote to Jan and she wrote back, and I could hear the slightest bit of resistance in her response. She and her husband, Ted, had by then hosted many a journalist in Flint and would be happy to do the same for me. But, she said, she had to admit to a fatigue with the carpetbaggers coming through and then writing about Flint as a carica-ture of itself and along the way getting their facts wrong.

I listened and hoped to avoid the pitfalls. Jan and Ted soon offered tips and leads and the rich perspective of longtime resident-observers. It was Ted who said early on that there were two economies in Flint, the usual kind of economy that collapsed in Flint during the last few decades, as well as an economy of the heart, as he called it. In his travels around town, from bank to market to barber shop, random strangers traveled as his fellow Flintstones. Jan, meanwhile, generously offered the tools of a veteran journalist, with lists of local authors and their works, back issues of her astute and newsy *East Village Magazine*, a series of her own stories on local notable people in Flint, and her frank and valuable insights.

On my first visit I drove directly to the water treatment plant, where I saw that the barrier arm near the front gate was broken off. I drove through and then around the buildings, noting the drums of chemicals up against the walls. Soon an employee in a plant truck drove alongside me. I rolled down the window. He said I'd have to leave. He saw my camera and said I could get a better photo from the vantage point of the scrap yard next door. I drove into the scrap yard parking lot and pointed my camera out the window until the owner ran out and ordered me to leave.

On my next visit to Flint, I made a point of spending a day going to places overlooked in the "worst of" stories. I started out at the Flint Institute of Arts, the second-largest art museum in the state. I visited the Flint Farmers' Market, with its stalls of artisanal produce and ethnic foods to go. I went to the bookstore, to GoodBoy Clothing, and to several newer coffee shops and restaurants downtown. On that day I also looked up the most expensive houses for sale in Flint and found some curving streets and stately manses that looked like the homes of suburban Detroit auto barons. As I took pictures in one particular neighborhood adjacent to a golf course on the west side of town, a woman drove up next to me, rolled down her window, and asked, "May I help you?"

The more I visited, the more I saw the boundaries and dualities of Flint. During the summer of 2018 I learned about an annual dance concert of drill teams to be held at Northwestern High School in Flint. There, in a polished gymnasium, some five hundred people watched a series of synchronized and choreographed routines by students who had practiced for months. The show honored an outgoing team coach and mentor as well as some graduating seniors who were heading off to an array of colleges, some with hefty scholarships.

I later learned about another large event that had taken place a night earlier, this one downtown, at the renovated Capitol Theater, where a sold-out crowd heard a live taping of the *Moth* radio hour, a storytelling show airing on public radio. When I asked an attendee about the racial composition of the crowd, I learned that it was nearly all white. The dance show had been nearly all black.

A few weeks later I was invited along on a guided bus tour through Flint, conducted by a resident who had been certified as a guide by the county. Beginning at the impressive downtown cultural center, we wound through wealthy, working-class, middle-class, and poor neighborhoods. We passed shuttered schools, open liquor stores, and torn-down residential blocks. Our tour guides described how so-called urban renewal in Flint had destroyed the two main black neighborhoods with a freeway now running through each. The guides, too, complained about the negative representations of Flint in the media, referring to stories about poverty, crime, or water.

At the end of the trip I queried some passengers, a group of very inquisitive University of Michigan students who had matriculated from many parts of the country and were here to study public health. In informal interviews they each expressed upset. Why so many liquor stores? Why the shuttered schools? The burned-down houses? Where did people work? Was Flint *really* making the comeback that these students had heard about in the classroom?

If they had visited a year later, though, they might have seen signs. On the north side, where rows of blighted properties had looked postapocalyptic, land bank crews were clearing the landscape of ruin, replacing destruction with fields of grass. These sites looked better than before, no matter what they were to become. Downtown, construction of an expansive new nonprofit K–8 charter school was underway. The two-story Flint Cultural Center Academy was being built through a donation by the Charles Stewart Mott Foundation, and the school will adjoin the Flint Institute of Music. Students will spend a part of every day at other facilities on the Flint Cultural Center campus, which include the art and music institutes, a planetarium, a performing arts theater, and a public library. It sounded like the enrichments available to wealthy, tuition-paying New York or San Francisco families. Here it would be free to families in Flint, if chosen in a lottery.

During each of my visits to Flint I met with a group of young people, usually over very large meals. At a roadhouse one fifteen-year-old polished off a twenty-two-ounce porterhouse steak, two orders of fries, and dessert. We went to all-you-can-eat buffets and to Tony's in Frankenmuth, just off the freeway north of Flint, where the sign welcomed deer hunters and single portions were large enough for a party of eight. Tony's BLT was served with one pound of bacon. Our table of five was unable to finish the Tony's Special Sundae, a tower of ice cream, brownies, chocolate, whipped cream, and cherries.

During those meals we talked about ordinary teen topics and those specific to Flint: grades, college, careers, parents, buses, bicycles, cops, guns, racism, cars, growing up with the stigma of Flint, and the hassles of Flint's water. I realized that the Flint water crisis was both central to daily life and also, because of its routine, now a part of the background. As the year wore on, I noticed shifts in points of view, as a group of fifteen-year-olds turned sixteen, got jobs, passed driver tests, and bought cars. Adulthood comes early in Flint.

I went to other institutions and meetings in Flint, once to a meeting of neighborhood groups at Applewood, the old estate and gentleman's farm belonging to the Mott family. One night I went to the Sloan Museum to see the exhibit *An Equal Opportunity Lie*, the story of segregation and discrimination in Flint's housing. I stayed for a lecture, part of a series by the Flint Truth and Action Partnership Project, a national initiative funded by the W.K. Kellogg Foundation to promote racial healing. Dr. Erica Britt, a linguist at the University of Michigan–Flint and a newcomer to Flint, presented lively recordings from her Vehicle City Voices project and described a once-thriving Flint, though one with sharp racial separations.

My trips to Flint included talks with families, storekeepers, baristas, journalists, and academics. I met Jiquanda Johnson, a Flint native, journalist, and champion of Flint youth. During the water crisis she watched out-of-town reporters write about Flint in a way that she didn't always recognize. Johnson left her job at the *Flint Journal* to start her own online news site, Flint

Beat, which tracks Flint issues. She partnered with the Trace, a national news site dedicated to covering youth gun violence, an epidemic in Flint. Johnson organized a journalism project with Flint youth, training them in writing and reporting to participate in a national project, Since Parkland, which chronicled youth gun deaths after the horrific Parkland shootings.

Flint had enough facets and textures that I could have kept filling notebooks. But it was time to find a way to weave all the disparate parts together. I was, of course, overwhelmed. Discovery was absorbing, consuming. Writing? Less so. By then, the coming-together-of-diverse-groups narrative had shifted into something more complex. There were disputes about who deserved credit and how safe the water was. And Flint itself was far more multifaceted than the "Murdertown, USA" headline in the *New York Times Magazine*.

At first I tried to let the many teen conversations that took place over megameals guide the book. It was where I started, anyway. Why shouldn't youth tell a story for youth? Excellent and clear-headed editors, though, soon reminded me about a storyteller's closest friend: time. I needed to stick with chronology. And so I started at the beginning and tried to let the flow of the water guide the shape of the story.

And then came Newark, about six and a half miles from my New Jersey town, according to Google. Could there be a better example of what Flint had been saying all along—Flint is a sentinel; Flint tells the story of America; the nation must listen to Flint. Newark confirmed that any post-industrial city in the US could face what Flint is facing. And Flint had told the world that when it does the voices of people must come together and roar. They must bellow loudly. They must insist and persist. Flint has taught the world that, like freedom, clean water is our basic human right. Flint had said it plainly in a public art project on display in a chain-link fence on Flint's north side. Water bottles poking through the links spelled out a phrase: water is life.

—Candy J. Cooper

Acknowledgments

Writing a book can feel like one person alone in a room. With this book I learned that it can expand into a crowd in a great hall. I want to thank the young adults in Flint who helped me to understand what life feels like growing up in their city: Whitney Frierson, Derrick Washington, Ty Belin, Delante Mckenney, Marquez Williams, Montae Cherry, Keishaun Wade, Ny'Azia Johnson, and Earl Hall, among many others.

The editor who guided this project, Susan Dobinick at Bloomsbury, offered early enthusiasm that fed my own. Her fine judgment at the right moments elevated everything. I am also indebted to close, careful copy editing by Diane Aronson and Hattie LeFavour at Bloomsbury, and design work by Elizabeth Lindy, John Candell, and Donna Mark. Erin Cox offered sharp judgment and guidance in the transition from asking to answering questions.

Thank you to Paul Herring, whose company, Spectacle TV, records Flint City Council meetings, enabling researchers to see and link together the very long chain of Flint citizen concerns. Rick Sadler helped point me to data while debunking myths. Michelle Swanson checked my water facts. Carma Lewis offered insight into Flint factions—with kindness and a great laugh. Jiquanda

Johnson, who started *Flint Beat*, kept me up-to-date on Flint news that mattered. Big thanks to Jan Worth-Nelson and Ted Nelson—and to the staff of *East Village Magazine* for sophisticated local journalism. Ben Pauli helped with perspective and information. The late Jackie King, a martial arts master and Flint icon, offered stories about Flint youth and history even as he battled illness. He died in December of 2018.

Other help came from Nick Delbanco, who advised correctly, and Frank Albanese, whose advice at a tense moment eased outsized worries. Woody Roberts served as a news alert system. Tom Henderson shared his stories of Flint entrepreneurship from *Crain's Detroit*. David Zeman, editor of *Bridge Magazine*, said yes. Mike Gillis roamed photo files in Grand Rapids. Brittany Greeson was patient and generous. Valerie Wojciechowski donated her photographs. Jacqueline Combs-Nelson accompanied me on a day of reporting with warmth and astute observation. Antonia Kaz tracked down permissions with dispatch. My cousin and namesake, Candy Crowley, served as my personal Yaddo but was, I am certain, more fun. She offered solitude when I most needed it, along with steadfast news sense, abundant wisdom, and crucial hilarity. My sister, Holly Wolff, a choral singer, led me to Andrea Ramsey, the composer. Other family—Heather, Sarah, Howard, Karen, Dave—have been super-promoters.

My companion on my first visit to Flint for this project was my late father, Howard Cooper. Together we stormed the water treatment plant and got kicked out of the nearby scrapyard while he told stories about Billy Durant and J. Dallas Dort and the birth of General Motors. Later in life he married Anne, a former Flint resident and Flint enthusiast. Together my father and Anne became power listeners, connectors, and cheerleaders. My father died during the making of this book. I so wish he could have seen what he helped to launch.

Thanks to Elly Meeks, who unfailingly said it all sounded great, as did Kathy Seligman from afar. Toni Martin took over for me at Succeed2gether, a fine after-school tutoring program in Montclair, New Jersey. My twenty-three-year-old writer's group started this project when Marina Budhos, a novelist, connected me with her husband, Marc Aronson, a wizard-like conceptualist in young adult nonfiction. Marc kept the whole forest in focus while I wandered the understory. Thank you, thank you to both.

That takes me to my closest beloveds, my family. My husband, Bob Weisbuch, was left to manage at home with my adored son, Gabriel. Bob, especially, witnessed the making of this book. Like others in the crowd in the great hall, he believes in saying yes—to a vital story that needs to be told. I owe him a magnum of my finest thank-yous.

Credits and Contributors

Poem on vii: By and used with the permission of Jonah Mixon-Webster. Originally published in *Stereo(TYPE)*, Ahsahta Press, 2018.

Jonah Mixon-Webster is a poet and conceptual/sound artist from Flint, Michigan. His debut poetry collection, *Stereo(TYPE)*, won the 2017 Sawtooth Poetry Prize from Ahsahta Press, the 2019 PEN America/Joyce Osterweil Award, and was a finalist for the 2019 Lambda Literary Award for Gay Poetry. He is an assistant professor of English at Lansing Community College, and he is completing his PhD at Illinois State University.

Maps on p. xi: map of Flint: © 2020 Digital Vector Maps; inset map of Michigan and the Great Lakes: iStock.com/pavalena.

Photographs on 8, 30, 37, 39, 58, 66 [all], 68, 72, 86, 88 [all], 96, 111, 118, 120, 126–127, 132, 150, 153, 170 (top), 176, 186, 188, 196: By and used with the permission of Brittany Greeson.

Brittany Greeson is a Detroit-based independent photographer. Her work has appeared in the *New York Times*, the *Washington Post*, the *Wall*

Street Journal, Time, The Atlantic, and many other publications. She was named the 2017 Michigan Press Photographer of the Year. She specializes in documenting American daily life, including issues of socioeconomic and gender inequality.

Photographs on 20, 32, 71, 74, 93, 156, 164, 178, 181, 212, 220: by Jake May and used with the permission of MLive.

Jake May, chief photographer for the *Flint Journal,* was a 2017 Pulitzer Prize finalist in Feature Photography. He also received the 2016 Society of Professional Journalists' Sigma Delta Chi Award in Feature Photography for his work documenting the Flint water crisis. In 2018, May was named Small Market Photographer of the Year by the National Press Photographers Association, which also awarded him a special citation for his work on the Flint water crisis.

Photograph on 24: by Samuel Wilson and used with the permission of MLive.

Samuel Wilson is an independent photojournalist and filmmaker based in Portland, Oregon. He is interested in the ways communities, large and small, develop identity over time.

Photograph on 46: by Ryan Garza and used with the permission of Detroit Free Press via ZUMA Wire.

Ryan Garza, who was born and raised in Flint, worked for more than a decade as a staff photographer for the *Flint Journal* before joining the *Detroit Free Press* in 2012. He has won numerous state and national awards, including an Edward R. Murrow award for his work documenting the Flint water crisis. Garza was named Michigan Press Photographer of the Year in 2012.

Image on 56: courtesy of Huntington Library.

Graphic on 78: by Milton Klingensmith; used with the permission of MLive.

Photographs on 82, 170 (bottom), 198, 202: by and used with the permission of Valerie Wojciechowski.

Valerie Wojciechowski, a native of Burton, adjacent to Flint, grew up witnessing the struggles of Flint. She chose the water crisis as the subject of her senior thesis exhibit at Grand Valley State University, where she graduated in 2019 with a Bachelor of Arts in photography. She is an adjunct photographer for *Grand Valley Magazine* and other university publications.

Graphic on 99: courtesy of Centers for Disease Control and Prevention.

Documents on 108, 114: courtesy of Genessee County District Court Records.

Photograph on 146: by Regina H. Boone and used with the permission of *Detroit Free Press* via ZUMA Wire.

Regina H. Boone is a photojournalist for the *Richmond Free Press*, a weekly newspaper founded by her late father and owned by her family. Previously, she was a staff photographer for the *Detroit Free Press*, where she covered a wide range of stories, including the Flint water crisis. Her captivating photograph of two-year-old Sincere Smith of Flint became an iconic image of the crisis.

Photograph on 199: by Sammy Jo Hester and used with the permission of MLive.

Sammy Jo Hester is the first women's sports photo editor at the *Los Angeles Times*. A 2014 graduate of Western Kentucky University's photojournalism program, Hester worked as a photographer at the *Flint Journal* and as a photo editor at the *Daily Herald* in Provo, Utah.

Lyrical composition on pages 216–218 by and used with the permission of Andrea Ramsey. Sheet music copyright 2017 by G. Schirmer, Inc. International copyright secured. All rights reserved.

Andrea Ramsey is an award-winning composer, conductor, scholar, and music educator. A native of Arkansas, she has held positions in music education and conducting at Ohio State University and University of Colorado. She has also conducted children, youth, and young adult choirs around the country. Now a full-time composer and guest conductor, Ramsey has written some one hundred works to date. Her composition about the Flint water crisis, "But a Flint Holds Fire," has been performed by youth and young adult choirs throughout the country.

Index